• • •

Value To Others

June 2017

Value To Others

52 insights into business and personal success

Dr. Chris Mason

ISBN: 1542983347
ISBN-13: 9781542983341
Library of Congress Control Number: 2017901941
Melbourne, Victoria, Australia

Contents

Introduction–Getting Started

Whether you own a business, work for someone else, or plan to start a business, there are some key success factors you need to know. Generally, these things are not taught at a university or even on the job, yet they are all important and easy to learn. I wrote this book in part because when I stepped into my first CEO role in 1985, I naively thought I would get support from my board, but I got none. I have been trying to support other leaders ever since, and I sincerely hope you will find this book supportive in your own leadership role, whatever that may be.

It makes no difference what type of organization you are leading; the core success factors are the same. There is one important difference, however, and that is *you*. You have unique strengths, and this book will enable you to identify each one of them. You also have areas you need to work on, and I will show you how to do that as well. The plan for your business will be unique because it will be developed around you and your team.

Once you have identified your priorities, you will know exactly what to focus on, and—more importantly—you will know what to say no to. Most people feel bad saying no and end up taking on too much and not doing anything well. I have a great life because at any time, I know which three things in my business are the most strategic, and I make sure that I work on those things on most days. As I complete one of them, I can take on the next most important strategic issue.

The following chapters outline the fifty-two values and activities that you should consider for inclusion in your plan. You can read them in any order you like. At the end of each chapter is a short summary plus an area where you can record your current performance on that issue and make some notes. I suggest you read one chapter per week.

Each chapter is concise and easy to read. If you just want to read the book for good ideas and leave completing the plan for later, that works as well. You can focus on yourself, your business, or your specific part of the business. This can be an entertaining read or a strategic plan for your business—it's up to you. The aim of this book, as the title suggests, is to provide you with what we at Mindshop call "value to others" (VTO). Mindshop currently supports more than one thousand people and directly and indirectly supports thousands of organizations. Because VTO is one of the core values of Mindshop, we provide our people with all the tools, training, support, technologies, and networking they need to enable them to grow a successful business.

If you would like to arrange for some help with your plan or to share some feedback on the book, you can e-mail us at VTO@mindshop.com. You have invested money and are about to invest time in your future, which is the best place to make an investment. Take it seriously, do the work, read each of your key chapters several times, and continuously refine your one-page plan. I wish I could be there personally to guide you, but this is the next best thing.

Dr. Chris Mason
Founder and Chairman
Mindshop—www.mindshop.com
Melbourne, Australia
April 2017

Chapter 1

●　●　●

Value to Others

When you study the successful organizations and leaders of the world, you will always find this key success factor: each has a strong focus on core values. Mindshop has five core values, but the one we are best known for is value to others (VTO). In a nutshell, VTO means that if you focus on the needs of others, you increase your personal feeling of self-worth; if your self-worth is high, you are less likely to sabotage yourself; and if you reduce your self-sabotaging behavior, your personal success will increase. Most people understand this philosophy, but they fail to implement it. They may try it for a few days, but it takes years before VTO kicks in. Imagine that your self-worth is like a bank account: every time you do something for another person, it adds to your balance. And that balance is required to overcome your feeling of not being worthy. Where does this feeling of unworthiness come from?

Think about the people in your life you believe. When you were young, you probably believed your parents, teachers, and some of your friends. If they made statements such as "You have to work hard to be rich" or "You are hopeless at drawing," you probably believed them. Whom do you believe today? What do you believe today? We become hardened by life experiences, and we become more cynical about life as we grow older. See how many of the following statements you agree with:

* I'm not good at time management.
* I can't save my money.
* My fitness level has dropped as I've aged.
* I'm not skilled enough to run my own business.
* I can't speak in public.
* I'm going to retire at sixty.
* I'll never find the right life partner.
* I don't take risks.
* I can't trust strangers.
* I can't sell.

How many of these statements did you agree with? Where did each belief come from? If you agreed with "I can't save my money," is this a belief you came up with, or did someone tell you that you are incapable of saving?

If you agree with any of these statements, you will feel less worthy of success. When you reflect on situations in your life where you were close to succeeding, what happened? Did you do something to sabotage yourself? Was it a job promotion, a relationship, a competition, or even your weight that was the issue?

The good news is that I have a solution for avoiding self-sabotage. By focusing on the other person (VTO), you can feel good about yourself. For example, if you found a wallet and decided to hand it in at the local police station, how would that make you feel? Upon finding the wallet, many would think things like "The police will keep it" or "If the person was stupid enough to lose it, then he or she deserves to not have it" or even "I need it more than someone else does." The likely outcome is that you would keep the money for yourself, but what does that do for you in the long term?

I would hand the wallet over to the police, not caring what they did with it. I would do it for me, because I believe handing it in is the right outcome. I would feel proud of myself for handing it in; it is irrelevant what happens to it after that. It was this thinking that led me to the VTO philosophy.

Let me give you an example from my own experience. Around 1990 I met Kevin and Carol O'Brien, who ran a company called Cherry Berry Jams. They wanted my help in selling their business. Their accountant had valued the business at such a low price that he recommended against selling. When they asked me to value the business, I came up with a figure around six times that of the accountant's. Obviously, Kevin and Carol liked my figure, so they asked me to handle the sale and offered me a commission of 10 percent of the sale price. After a few months, the business sold at my figure, and it came time to pay me. I had invested only a few hours in the project and felt that the commission was not appropriate for the effort I had made. My other option was to charge them for the actual time, but that would have been such a small amount that my response was to say, "Forget it; there is no charge."

I believed that not charging the O'Briens was more than the right outcome; it was the right thing to do. This is probably not what the average person would have done, but I was brought up to do what is right and not be average. I thought at the time that I would get the commission back many times over—not from Kevin and Carol, but because I felt worthy of success, and it was an investment.

I have honed the concept over the years and now look for ways I can add VTO. It has driven the Mindshop business model, determined how we recruit and retain staff and clients, and shaped how I treat everyone around me, even strangers.

What stops most people from following this philosophy is the time lag between providing VTO and getting the reward. I always say the time lag is, on average, ten years. It takes a long time to build up the self-worth bank balance, but once it reaches a certain point, the rewards start trickling out. As you practice more and more VTO, the trickle grows to a stream and ultimately a flood. Priming the pump is the key. You can start today.

What You Can Do Today—Value to Others

1. Make a list of all the key people in your life—family, friends, customers, and colleagues.
2. Think about each person, and next to each name, write one thing he or she would find of value. It may be a family member, for instance, and the thing you could do for him is to share more quality time.
3. Develop a simple action plan you could do today to make it happen for three people on your list. Pick another three for tomorrow, and so on. Make this a habit. Your reward in the short term is a warm feeling for doing the right thing; in the long term, you will achieve personal and business success.

Chapter 2

●　　●　　●

Make the Complex Simple

We love complexity: it engages us and stimulates the intellectual side of our brains. It's a challenge to understand the complex. If it's too simple, there is something wrong with it. At Mindshop we are known for making the complex simple. As the founder of the company, I think this is in part due to me. I am a simple person; I struggle with the complex. Once I have worked through the struggle and worked out the answer, I try to make it simple for the next person. Even though I did not have things explained to me well, I managed to progress quickly up the organization as I learned to look at the big picture rather than get caught up in the details. It was a little like playing chess, where I could see the game unfolding five moves ahead. I'm not sure where that came from (perhaps it was in my DNA), but I still have that ability today. I look at the complex with my special five-moves-ahead glasses on, and it all looks simple.

I intuit the answer and then work out how I can explain it simply to others. I am a visual learner: I think in pictures and diagrams. So, I need to see it to explain it—hence our company's use of models and videos to share our knowledge. Most things in life can be complex. When driving a car, for instance, a lot of things are going on around us—other cars moving, pedestrians, changing road conditions—and our senses and brains take it all in. We can't think about everything, but our brains filter everything and bring to our attention the most important information so that we can make decisions about what to do next.

Even then we may not be conscious of all the decisions, but the result is that we can get from point A to point B safely and efficiently. We are taught to drive a car, we need a license to prove we have passed a minimum standard of competency, and we believe that as we drive more and our experience grows, our proficiency increases. What about other parts of our life, such as relationships and business? They can be even more complex. How can we distill what is happening so that we can focus on the most important aspects?

In business we normally receive training—it may have been a business degree—but how relevant is that training to working in or running a business? My business degree didn't have much relevance to what I needed to know to run a public company. When I started my first job in 1968, I was not given any formal training. I was assigned to a more experienced person who directed me on my day-to-day tasks. No one explained the philosophy behind what we did, encouraged me to continuously suggest improvements, or set "stretch" goals for me. I was taught a combination of good and bad habits, but I couldn't really tell the difference at age seventeen.

When developing the strategy for a $300 million piece of business, the level of difficulty was no different than that of a business with less than $1 million in sales. It is simple. We know our products. We know the price at which they will sell in preference to those of our competitors. We know what profit we need to reward the shareholders. And we know we have to provide the goods or services. Now, that's not hard.

To beat your competitors, you need to consistently provide more value for the money while keeping your promises about service, quality, and on-time delivery. That's not hard. To keep your staff, you need to show them how they can use your company to achieve their goals and to grow their skills and confidence. That's not hard, either.

Think about the meetings you attend each day. Do the participants talk about how to do these things? Probably not. The meetings I used to go to when I was working for large organizations were very political. A lot of games were played, and your survival was linked to how well you played them. Later in life, when I was invited to be on corporate boards, I set some ground rules to minimize the game playing. At board meetings we had thirty minutes to deal with the operational issues; the rest of the time we needed to talk about and decide on strategy. If not, I would leave the meeting.

Even today I can't get excited over details. I like to rise above them and see the big picture; it is much simpler and more rewarding. The Mindshop tools we provide to our clients encourage either strategic thinking or efficient problem solving. The aim is to remove the noise we get from random conversations. Our discussions are structured, and the tools enable us to simply focus on the core problems rather than the symptoms of the problems.

All good leaders have the ability to cut to the chase, to keep it simple. They pick their words, and what they say is worth listening to. What they write is also focused: a few paragraphs of enlightened conversation that touch the emotions in us. You know when you read or hear those words that they are enlightened, and often you have to admit that you couldn't have said or written them that way. It has been said that it takes more time to craft a short answer than a long one; the inference is that it takes more time, but the outcome is better for it.

What You Can Do Today—Make the Complex Simple

1. You can start by writing a one-page plan. The plan should summarize where you are today, where you want to be in the future, and how you are going to get there.
2. Develop your strategies and action plans to solve your problems.

3. Think about what you write and what you say. Draft it, and then look for ways you can keep it simple.
4. Review everything you do, and look for ways to reduce complexity. Set a goal to reduce the steps of everything you do by half. You will be surprised to find that in most cases you can.

Chapter 3

● ● ●

Don't Retire

In the sixties and seventies, I worked for the government. The retirement age then was sixty-five. I worked with several people who had more than forty years of service, worked right up to their sixty-fifth birthday, retired, and then died within three months. I remember one guy, however, who couldn't wait until he reached sixty-five so that he could work on his family history. He kept on living and enjoying his retirement because he had something to live for.

I always say I'm going to work till I'm ninety-two; what will change every three to five years is the type of work I'll be doing—not me. The key is to stay passionate about life, and work is a vital component of the passion.

I handed over the day-to-day running of Mindshop to my eldest son, James, when he was only twenty-two. My logic at the time was that he would do a better job than I, and it would free me up to do different things. I have always felt that it is a bad idea to take your most experienced person and have him or her focus on the daily operations of a business, yet that is what happens in most organizations. Although you make money from effective operations, you make more money from great strategies backed up with effective operations.

Many people in their late fifties can't wait to retire so that they can do all the things they never made time for: sailing, traveling, studying, golf, and the like. They get burned out and feel they just can't go on. The thought of going to my retirement age of ninety-two seems completely off the planet to them. With life expectancy on the rise, I wonder how they will fund their retirement years. Many people I know retire, and within a few years, they become bored, having ticked off any bucket list items they could afford. (They rationalize that they don't want all the other bucket list items anymore.) My plan is to not retire, keep earning well into my nineties, and weave my bucket list items into my day-to-day activities—a fully integrated life.

My view is that you need to keep reengineering yourself and your job so that you leverage your strengths and keep learning. One of my bosses in the government once said to me, "If a person thinks his education is finished, then he is finished." It's a catchy saying, but it's also true. I aim to reengineer myself at least once a year. Every November I start thinking about what I am enjoying and what I am not. I overlay that list with what I could delegate or stop doing.

My challenge is to create a 50 percent vacuum in my working life; it's a little like clearing out your garage once a year and creating space. Over the following year, the vacuum gets filled with stuff—both the strategic and the fun stuff. By the following November, some of it has become stale or boring, so it's time to clean it out again.

Leadership is all about taking on new jobs (which you probably hate doing at the start), making them things you love, delegating those things you love to someone else, and then taking on more things you hate and repeating the cycle. Those people who find leadership difficult usually find it difficult to delegate, preferring to keep the tasks to themselves. Each year becomes more of the same. They justify keeping these tasks with thoughts like "It is easier to do it myself" and "I don't have anyone I can delegate to, so I have no choice but to do it myself."

If your job is a constant challenge, then you will keep learning and growing. Work will be exciting, and you will always have energy to spare, no matter what your age. People will enjoy being in your company and will seek your advice. You will feel valued.

The main reason I have taken this path is something different again. I like technology, which is changing faster and faster. Back in my government days, I remember thinking that the rate of change was so great I wouldn't be able to keep up. I wished it would stay still for a while. I think just the opposite today. I wish it would move faster. My vision for Mindshop was developed around virtual reality as a delivery process. We will be waiting still longer before we get it, but in the meantime, Mindshop has been built for it. When it finally comes, we will have a structure that it will just slot into perfectly. I can't retire until I see this day.

Associated with this thinking is the issue of planning. Even with technology, there is a lot of research to do. The best person to do this research is the person with the widest perspective and a good understanding of the overall vision for the organization. The best person for this is an owner. Most owners are caught up in day-to-day operations. They have little, if any, time for research and stargazing. I have the time to think and plan, to research the emerging technologies, to subscribe to the technology blogs and websites, to build international relationships, and to network with people globally to find out what is happening in my markets.

My view is that the older, experienced people like me should be coaching the younger people with less experience but more potential. Most CEOs don't have time for any of these activities. I can't think of anything better to spend my time on. I have to delegate or stop doing my day-to-day jobs to make time to be strategic and innovative.

Retirement for me is at least fifteen to twenty-five years away. That's an exciting thought. Just think what I can achieve and the people I can help in that time! The most exciting aspect is what I will become over the next twenty-five years. I have grown so much over the past fifty, and the mind boggles about what I'll know, the people I'll know, how big Mindshop will be, and what will happen to my family. No way am I retiring. I don't want to miss any of this.

What You Can Do Today—Don't Retire

1. Look at how you can create a vacuum in your working life that you can fill with strategic and innovative tasks.
2. Stop thinking of retirement. Keep reengineering yourself and your job each year.

Chapter 4

● ● ●

Forgive Those Who Wrong You

As you go through life, you experience situations where other people do the wrong thing by you. You have a choice as to how you respond. What is the worst thing a person has done to you? Stolen your money? Spread rumors about you? Betrayed your trust? Not repaid a debt? I've experienced all these things myself. At first I felt wronged and angry. For example, if someone was slow in paying a debt, I started a process of sending warning letters and ultimately taking legal action to get my money. It didn't make me feel good, and I'm not sure it was financially a success because the time and energy required to recover the debts outweighed the benefits.

About twenty-five years ago, I decided I should forgive all my debtors. I made a list of all the people who owed me money and wrote each a personal letter saying, "Just wanted you to know I have written off the money you owe me, and I wish you well for the future." I sent out about twenty letters. I'm not sure how many reached my ex-clients, as some of the contact details were old and the people were experts in avoiding their creditors, but I didn't care.

I didn't do it for these people; I did it for me. Carrying the emotional debt cost me energy. I remember running into one of those ex-clients at a trade fair. I saw him at the stand where he was exhibiting his products. I really hadn't given him a thought since I sent him my letter, but I can only assume he never got it because when he spotted me in the crowd, he vanished in an instant. I thought at the time what a price he was paying emotionally by not paying his debts.

The other reason for forgiving people who wrong you is that you yourself may be wrong! If someone doesn't pay you as promised after you have sent an invoice, then you are clearly in the right. But what about those occasions when the "wrong" is less clear? I had a situation where I had employed someone to play a particular role, and I perceived that this person had let me down by doing a poor job, costing me more money than all the bad debts in the history of Mindshop. I remember sitting with this guy and debating what had happened, me telling my version of the events, him countering with his version. We were getting nowhere. I then said to him, "I have listened to your version, and it is wrong!" He responded defensively, and I added, "My version is also wrong. We will never know what really happened. The truth is lost; we only have our versions, both of which are wrong. So let's just talk about what we will do in the future." It was a major lesson for me. I have learned not to believe my memory and to equally value the other person's version of events as I do mine.

I now look back on this situation and others like it, and I want to thank these individuals for their contributions. Every event, whether perceived as positive or negative, has contributed to where our company is today and where we are heading. By adopting the philosophy of "forgive all those who have wronged you" (and those you *perceive* have wronged you), you are safe.

The key is to move on and not worry about the past. My biggest test was when we experienced an employee embezzling company funds. I am pleased to say, my philosophy withstood the test. It was a large amount of money at the time, but my instant reaction was to think, "There is an opportunity here; where is it?" When the police asked me what outcome I wanted, I said that I wanted the person convicted of theft but saw no value in jail time, and that was exactly the outcome we got. Was I disappointed in not getting any of the money the court awarded us? No! For me, disappointment results when the outcomes and the expectations are different. I expected none of the money to be returned, so I wasn't disappointed.

In a strange way, forgiving wrongs like this is practicing value to others, as explained in chapter 1. It provides value to the other party. Determine how you can use the event to benefit yourself in the future in a way that doesn't hurt others, and you will have found your way forward. Every storm cloud has a silver lining; invest the time and energy in finding it.

Think about the wrongs you have experienced, and reflect on the ultimate benefit you got out of each. You should find that you have grown and benefited from each incident. What are the lessons for the future? Forgive everyone who has wronged you. Where possible, tell people you have forgiven them. Examine your version of each event, and ask yourself, "Am I seeing it right?" Forgive yourself for your part in the incident. That's right: forgive yourself for wronging yourself.

What You Can Do Today—Forgive Those Who Wrong You

1. Make a list of everyone who has wronged you. Examine your own role in each incident, and forgive yourself.
2. Contact each person to let him or her know you have moved on, and then move on.

Chapter 5

● ● ●

Recruit on Core Values

When you are growing or changing a business, recruitment is a key activity. The costs of getting it wrong are high. Most people recruit based on skills, qualifications, and relevant experience. At Mindshop we recruit on core values because we believe that we can't change the way your parents brought you up, but we can train you in everything else.

If you recruit on skills, qualifications, and experience, it determines the whole recruitment process—that is, the questions you ask and the decision you ultimately make. If you recruit on core values, it's a different process, with different questions and different outcomes. The reason traditional recruitment focuses on the tangible things is that it is much easier to do. Recruitment based on core values is more difficult.

If your core values include broad headings such as "service," "quality," and "communication," then it makes sense that anyone you employ will believe in and practice those values. The challenge is how to establish this in an interview situation. You could ask a question like, "Do you have good customer service skills?" but it is likely the applicant will say yes, so where do you go from there? You could always consult the applicant's references and ask, "Does this person practice good customer service?" but again, it is most likely that the person will answer with a standard yes.

This difficulty is the reason why the standard interview process uses questions such as "How many years did you work for company X?" or "Do you have any qualifications in marketing?" If the candidate worked for company X for many years and also completed a marketing degree, then you hope he or she will be good at customer service, but this is a big assumption to make.

I suggest a couple of alternative things you could do to test for the core value of customer service. How about asking during the interview, "What would you do if a customer wanted to return a product?" The average person will say, "I would ask my supervisor what our policy is for returning products." The person with exceptional customer service values may say, "If the product was undamaged, I would offer to exchange the product or refund the money and check later what our policy is on returns."

You may be thinking that a young person with limited experience is unlikely to respond in the way I am suggesting. My argument is that a person with the right core values would because it is how he or she would expect to be treated by an exceptional company. You could always test this, of course, by asking an intermediary question of the average person in the previous example. For instance, you could then say, "If your supervisor was not available, what would you do?" I feel that this question weakens the whole process, but you will still have an indicator you can use in the interview.

Core values come from a person's upbringing, not training. I remember a full-page advertisement for a hotel chain in an American newspaper that said, in part, "We don't train our people to be nice; we just hire nice people." You can always design clever questions to test any core values, but even then, the problem of the interview process being unnatural remains. What you could do is put the final contenders for a position through a real situation.

If you want to know how well they handle situations where customer service is needed, then put them in such a situation. You could even test them with a "secret shopper" so you can witness firsthand how they handle themselves under pressure. Some of you might think this approach is unfair, but I'd argue it is of value to all concerned.

If an applicant is not successful, he or she will benefit from the learning experience that it provides. The successful applicant will benefit not just because she wins the job, but because she knows she won it based on her core values, a worthy win. As the employer, you also win because you minimize the probability of making an employment error.

The time and effort required to interview on core values are greater, but the higher quality of the employees you hire makes it all worthwhile. Your people are your organization, and the most important role of any leader is to build a cohesive and integrated team.

At Mindshop we use this approach and have extended it to how we "hire" our customers. We hire our customers based on core values. Keep in mind that we are not a retailer or a manufacturer; we manage networks of people and deliver a desired outcome. Around 50 percent of the value we provide to our network members comes from us: our intellectual property, our management of conferences, and our coaching. The other 50 percent comes from the network itself, and the bottom line is that we need to manage both in similar ways, even recruiting people.

What You Can Do Today—Recruit on Core Values

1. Make a list of your core values.
2. Develop questions that you can ask potential employees that will test their belief in and application of each of your core values.

3. Design practical exercises that you can use to see how your applicants apply these values.
4. Consider developing a similar approach for recruiting your customers.

Chapter 6

●　　●　　●

Aim for a Win-Win

If you have just finished an enjoyable meal in a restaurant and have been presented with the bill, you would leave a tip for the person who served you. How do you decide how much the tip should be? I normally calculate what 10 percent of the bill is and then reflect on how good the overall experience was—the food, the service—and often a couple of figures come to mind. When that happens, I automatically choose the highest figure for the tip. I always want the other person to benefit.

What about when you are buying a major item like a house or a car? Do you negotiate to the point where the other person will go no further? I don't. I go into the purchase of any major item with a win-win outcome in mind. In the case of buying a car, I have a rough idea through my prior research of the margin available to the car retailer. I also value my time. I want a fair price in the minimum amount of time. I also say to the salesperson at the start of the process that I am going to get two quotes, and whoever comes up with the best price will get my business.

Once I agree on the price, I always say, "I know you have a bit more you could give me, but I want you to be happy with the deal." I then expect the salesperson to give me a bit more service. It's a little like giving the person who serves you in a restaurant the tip before your meal. I've actually done that, but it isn't my normal practice in a restaurant. However, it is when I buy a car.

With a big item like a house, I think it is even easier. I know the seller asks more than he expects to get, so there is probably a margin of around 5 percent in the price for negotiation. I do my research via the web and get a feel for the market. I know if I can get the house I want for 5 percent less than the asking price, I consider it to be a good outcome for me and figure that I'm probably meeting the price at which the seller will be happy. (I'll never know the thought process of the seller because normally you never meet sellers when you buy through an agent.)

With the last house we bought, we worked out a price (which was about 5 percent under the asking price), told the agent we would buy it for that price if some pots (you'll see why we included this slightly odd request in just a moment) and a kitchen appliance were included in the deal, and waited. I made it clear there was no flexibility in the price. I also said that if the seller wouldn't accept the price, there was another house we would like to look at. I made it clear to him that our offer was a final one and that we would move on if it wasn't enough for the seller.

The next step was some minor back-and-forth exchanges, at which time I conceded the pots and the appliance, none of which I really wanted in the first place. Once I agree on a deal, I never change my mind. I know the seller wants a smooth sale, and once we have agreed on a price, I will do everything in my power to make it a good experience for the other party. In our case, the seller was the person living next door to the house we bought, which was an even better reason for finding a win-win outcome.

Every day you need to make decisions like this: tipping at a restaurant, letting someone entering the freeway get in front of you, giving people time you had reserved for yourself, or giving up a parking space at the local shopping center. You may never see the person you benefit again, so why worry?

In a business situation, you are always faced with decisions about what to do with your time and money. For example, many people ignore e-mails and phone messages on the grounds that they are too busy to communicate with anyone who is not important to them. I answer all my e-mails, except those that are obviously spam. When someone I don't know sends me some product information, I have three choices: ignore it, toss it, or reply. Which response provides the best value to the other person? Obviously, the last one, and what does it cost me? Maybe two minutes to say thank you but explain that I'm not interested.

Situations like tipping and replying to e-mails are an application of the "value to others" philosophy outlined in chapter 1. By giving value to others, you increase your self-worth, which reduces your self-sabotaging behavior, which then increases your success in all aspects of your life.

The bottom line is that I give to the other person because it makes me feel good.

What You Can Do Today—Aim for a Win-Win

1. Whenever you find yourself wondering which way to go in a decision, always decide in favor of the other person. Some of the situations where you may feel undecided include tipping, donating to charity, driving courteously, engaging in family time, and responding to e-mails and phone calls.
2. Practice finding ways that will benefit the other person for a week, and see what happens.

Chapter 7

●　　●　　●

Query Every Cost

I know it seems like a commonsense notion to query every cost, but you'd be surprised at the levels of waste present in all organizations. At Mindshop we believe there is around 20 percent waste that can be removed from most organizations, and the exciting part is that it all goes to the bottom line.

Profit is a measure of the efficiency of a business. If your price point is competitive and you are making an above-average profit, then you must be running the business efficiently. Back in the eighties, I did a lot of work in the automotive components manufacturing sector in Australia. There were some interesting lessons to be learned.

The large car manufacturers—such as General Motors, Toyota, and Nissan—had realized that around 75 percent of their costs were for components they outsourced. Up until then, they were in constant battles with their suppliers over pricing. I approached the purchasing director of Nissan and convinced him to introduce me to their suppliers so that we could assist them in removing the waste from their operations. In effect, what we did was to set the prices for components and deduct a fair profit, and what remained was the available amount to spend on the manufacture of the components.

This approach forces you to query every cost. I have always liked the definition of waste that goes something like this: "Waste is whatever the customer won't pay for." What this means is that you need to identify where value is added and query any other costs. For example, at Mindshop we constantly query travel costs. I didn't like it at first, and as the chairman, my thinking was that if I traveled from Melbourne to London for a meeting, I needed to go business class so that I arrived in the best shape possible. This thinking lasted for a while.

But in time, I looked at the extra cost of a trip when flying business class, multiplied it by the number of trips I took in a year, and saw that it was going to cost an extra $100,000 a year. Over ten years, that would be a million dollars! I thought of all the things a million dollars could buy and decided we couldn't justify business class (unless we could upgrade by using our frequent flyer miles). Over time, the airlines introduced much cheaper around-the-world business-class fares, and I returned to flying closer to the front of the plane, but for years we reaped the benefits of the savings.

We use the same logic when we consider hiring another staff member. If the average total cost of a person is, say, $70,000 a year and, on average, the person stays ten years; that is an investment of $700,000. I really think seriously before I spend that much money, and so should you.

On occasion, our people have felt a little overworked, and their automatic response is that we need more people. My counterargument goes like this: "You say you are busy, and I know you are. Twenty percent of what you do in an average workweek develops 80 percent of the value you are to Mindshop, which means 80 percent of what you do only contributes 20 percent of the value, so what things could we cut out?" Normally such a review frees up a quarter of that person's time. Do that with all your people, and you will create an extra person for every four people you currently have. Start the process with yourself!

One of the things that should be an opportunity for you is your budgeting process. Most people assume their sales will increase over the prior year by a certain percentage—let's say 10 percent. They then look at the expenses, particularly the variable costs, and assume they will go up by 10 percent as well. I believe you need to query every cost, so don't adopt a process where costs are automatically increased.

The best way to achieve cost savings is to take the previous year's expenditures by category and reduce the total cost by 10 percent. For example, if you spent $100,000 on travel, set a target for this year of $90,000. Now work backward and develop a plan to reduce the travel costs. You will find that it is just too hard to reduce costs in some categories; in others, you will find more savings than just 10 percent. Your aim is to reduce your costs by an average of 10 percent.

Encourage all your people to suggest ways that costs can be reduced. You may not like all the suggestions, but you will like the outcome if you can reduce your costs by 10 percent in this year and again the next. Your suppliers are part of your team, so ask them for ideas to reduce costs. Get into the habit of questioning every cost; your people will quickly realize that they need to put up cost-reduction suggestions and not cost-increasing ones.

What You Can Do Today—Query Every Cost

1. Make a list of all your costs, and work with your people to find ways to reduce each by 10 percent in the coming year. It is as simple as reviewing your financial accounts line by line and identifying the waste or inefficiencies. Your aim is to average 10 percent savings on each line, knowing that some items will be easier to reduce than others.
2. Talk to your suppliers, and get their help in reducing costs. They normally won't volunteer to do this, but once asked, they are a valuable source of ideas.

Chapter 8

● ● ●

Develop a Long-Term Vision

I remember meeting with a very senior person from our bank. He was signing off on a strategic alliance with Mindshop and wanted to get a feel for how professional we were. He asked me this simple question: "How far do you plan ahead?" He was probably expecting an answer like two years or perhaps even five. He was shocked when I responded forty-two years.

He laughed, so without pausing for breath, I reached into my papers and pulled out our 2040 plan. It was like a graph, an exponential curve on which were marked all the key events we had experienced in the past. These events resulted in us being where we were at that time, and the next forty-two years were marked with major factors that would push us to our vision.

Among those factors from the past were setting up the documentation of all our intellectual property on video and databases and establishing our UK presence. Factors in the future included expansion into the United States, global strategic alliances, successions plans, and the utilization of emerging technologies such as videoconferencing and, ultimately, virtual reality.

I calmly explained the plan, answering his questions as I went. He pushed back from his desk, looked me straight in the eye, and said, "We will work with you, but we must have some equity in Mindshop." I responded that we didn't do that. He wasn't perturbed by my answer, though, and agreed to work with us anyway.

As I left, he had one last question for me. "Why forty-two years?" My answer made him smile. "Because by then I'll probably be dead, and it will be someone else's problem!" (With the continuous improvement in health care, I have since revised the age at which I am likely to die by a few more years.)

The reason why having such a long-term vision works is that you know clearly what to say yes to and, more importantly, what to say no to. I probably say no to many more things than I say yes to. Initially, I felt bad doing this because I was brought up to believe that it's impolite to say no to people. With my vision clearly in focus, however, I have no choice.

I have been questioned as to why we have invested so heavily in growing international markets. The answer is, I need to be in the United Kingdom and North America for my plan to work. If I only wanted to focus on short-term cash, I would have focused only on the Australian market.

Once your purpose as a person or a business becomes clear, you become "on purpose," and everything falls naturally into place. The people you need to meet, the money you need to grow, and the products that will take you forward automatically appear just as they are needed. I believe they don't come early because they know they are coming; it's mere mortals like me who need constant reassurance that they are coming.

I have learned to trust my vision and my purpose. I am being guided in everything I do; even writing this book was meant to happen. You can only start to understand your life when you look back and connect the dots. I have kept diaries and journals since the seventies, and every now and again I read back over them. With the benefit of hindsight, I can see the magic of how it all fits together: why I married Julie; why we have three children; why I worked at the Newsprint Mill in Albury, New South Wales; why I missed out on that specific promotion; and so on.

It is comforting to know there is a plan; it makes life simple. I know that as long as I stay true to my vision, it will all work out perfectly. You can tell when you are on purpose because everything happens perfectly, and there are no struggles. When you move off purpose, you can also feel it; you start hitting barriers, and things start going wrong. As you move back on purpose, the synchronous things start happening again, and the speed at which things move cranks up again.

I guess what I have learned is that it's not so much about the destination; it's all about the journey. When I first started as a consultant, I believed that you needed to lock down the timing on everything. Over the past three decades, however, I have moved away from that belief. I no longer think the timings are important. Things happen in their own time when they are ready. I still teach people to set time lines, but I do so without conviction.

Today I am even more convinced of the importance of the vision minus timing. I constantly look at my vision, which means that my focus is not on the short term. Instead, I look a long way ahead, trusting myself to find the footing, knowing it will all work out fine. Most people wait until they can see every step of the plan before they take the first step. But they can never see enough steps, so they stay where they are and never move. They fail to get close to their potential, and deep down, they know it. They feel frustrated, thrashing around for answers, trying out everyone else's solutions. They go from one seminar to the next, looking for each guru's one good idea that will make them a success. I have learned there are no silver bullets. Tenacity is key.

The answer is already inside each of us. We can't find it because we are surrounded by noise and can't hear the little voice, the whisper, inside of us, calling out our vision. Part of what we do at Mindshop is to coach people to find their purpose and their vision, which is very rewarding. We can't take any credit because the answer was right in front of them all the time, but it is still rewarding all the same.

What You Can Do Today—Develop a Long-Term Vision

1. Decide today that you want a twenty-year vision, and start plotting what that looks like. (Draw it if you like, because, as they say, a picture is worth a thousand words.)
2. Look back over your life far enough so that you can identify the key events that have positively (and sometimes negatively) impacted you.
3. You can usually extrapolate from these events to see where you are heading and what your purpose and your vision will be.

Chapter 9

●　　●　　●

Growth Protects You

Where do you live? Listen to your answer. Mine is, "I am a world citizen based in Melbourne, Australia." I first wrote that in 1994 when I wrote my mission statement. My vision established that, for at least twenty years, I would be spending a large part of each year outside of Australia, but my love of travel wasn't the reason behind the vision. It was much more strategic.

When I worked at Laser Lab in 1985, we sold most of our products in the United States. Laser Lab was an international public company set up to leverage the ability of lasers to cut materials with very small tolerances, such as plastic and steel. We bought the most expensive component, the laser itself, in the States. This worked well because we also sold products in the United Kingdom, New Zealand, South Africa, and Australia and got paid in US dollars for much of our sales. We used them to pay our US supplier and so protected ourselves against currency-exchange variations. It was at this time I realized that you need global income to avoid a financial impact due to economic downturns in a specific market.

It's not just economic issues you need protection from. Many of Mindshop's current clients (and even more in the future) are global operators that want global support networks. Then we have the issue of intellectual property; we draw ours from all over the world. By traveling as much as we do, we learn what is working and not working in the countries we are visiting.

Another benefit of being truly global is image. People are impressed that you are successful globally; they know it is more difficult than being successful in your local market. It also puts pressure on you personally—pressure regarding who you are, how well you manage time, what you know, and what you can do.

All these factors come together to protect you. The bottom line is this: being a global organization is good for you. Why growth? How can growth protect you? It's all about overhead recovery. When you are not growing, you are likely to be consolidating. Consolidation is good in the short term, but it doesn't take you anywhere; it's just more of the same. Imagine if you could grow at 100 percent each year for five years. If you could, it would mean that in five years, you would be thirty-two times the size you are today. That's an interesting thought.

Let me ask you some questions. It is five years' time, and you are now thirty-two times bigger than you are today. Who are your customers? What products and services are you selling? Where are you located? How many of the original staff are still with you? What is your job? Aren't they good questions? I've left the best question till last. Who would want to work for you? See why growth is good? It doesn't have to be 100 percent compound growth for five years; even 20 percent compound growth for five years will have you almost two and a half times bigger than you are today (and the questions just outlined still work).

Do you have to target global growth? Not at all. Any growth is hard, but that's why you should do it. Your competitors won't have the courage to follow you. If they do, it will put them at risk, as it will you. If they follow you and do it well, they will be worthy competitors. We all need worthy competitors to keep us vigilant. You need to fund the growth; it costs a lot. You need to have the spare management capacity to drive the growth. It will take you twice as long and cost twice as much as you think. I still think it is a must-do activity.

What is your exit strategy? Let's assume you are a business owner. How and when will you exit? If you exit now and your business is in good shape, you may get a sale price of three to five times your average profit for the past three years. You can do the math on that one. What if you could get 100 percent or even 20 percent compound growth for the next three to five years and then exit? How much more money would you make over the next three to five years and then upon exit? Now do you believe me that growth is good?

If you did this on a global basis at the same time, you would significantly widen the net for potential buyers. You should find that if you are a globally growing business, instead of five times the profit, the multiplier may be seven, eight, or even ten times the profit. You can do the math for that scenario as well. Exciting stuff for any owner.

But I hear you saying you are not an owner, so none of this applies to you. I am encouraging you to start thinking like an owner, even if you are not one. Imagine if you acted like an owner for the next five years—what do you think will happen? Will your current boss appreciate it? What if you kept doing it anyway, for another five years, maybe? What I predict will happen to you is one of the following scenarios. Your boss will appreciate you and share the rewards with you. If your boss does not appreciate you, then someone else who does will spot you and offer you the chance to join him or her. Maybe you will buy or start your own business and become an owner. Whatever situation you find yourself in, growth protects you.

What You Can Do Today—Growth Protects You

1. Start learning how to make growth happen.
2. Search the web, read the books, follow thought leaders, complete the courses, and suggest to the people you work with that growth should be part of the business vision.
3. Become a student of growth and, in time, an expert in growth. You will be rewarded many times over for your efforts.

Chapter 10

● ● ●

Mistakes Are Valuable

How many mistakes do you make in a day? I once worked with a medium-size commercial printing company and found that it was about to go bust. I knew I had to do something fast, so I called a meeting of all the supervisors, around sixteen people. I started the meeting by asking them what the steps were in the value chain. I didn't word it like that; I actually said something like, "When the job comes from the sales department, what happens first? Then what happens? Then what happens?"

In this way, I drew up a flowchart of the process. It was hard for them. Each supervisor had a good idea of what happened in his or her section but little idea of how anyone else worked. After about two hours, we had created a flowchart showing how the work flowed from the time an order was placed until the customer received his or her goods. I then asked who the supervisor of the first step was, and a man with thirty-plus years of experience in the company put his hand up. I asked him how many mistakes a day were made in his section, and there was no way he was going to answer. We both just looked at each other for a few moments, which seemed like an eternity to everyone else in the room.

Eventually one of the other supervisors broke the silence. He said to the first supervisor, "Come on, Dave, remember the other day when you…" Before

Dave answered, I jumped in with, "Dave, this is not a witch hunt. I have no idea if it is four a day, six a day, or whatever."

With a grimace, Dave replied, "Probably four a day."

We all knew it was more, but I moved on with, "What is the average cost of one of your mistakes?" He had no idea—none of us did—so we sat down and worked it out, and to our surprise, it was only $100. I expected a lot more. The next and last question was, "How many days do you work a year, Dave?" He had no idea, but we quickly worked it out, and it was around 250 days. I then did the calculation: four mistakes a day, $100 a mistake, and 250 days meant that Dave created $100,000 a year in mistakes.

Dave was shocked, and my next question shocked everyone else: "Who is the supervisor of the second stage?" We then worked through the whole flowchart and calculated the waste due to mistakes. It came to almost $1.5 million. The room went quiet. While I had everyone's attention, I moved to the next stage of the process by asking Dave, "What sort of problems do you have to deal with when the job comes to you from the sales team?"

Now we couldn't stop Dave as he listed all his problems. I asked him to keep a simple record over the following week of the frequency of each problem. Every supervisor agreed to do the same. Can you see what was about to happen?

That night the supervisors crowded around the photocopier, copying their histograms, all keen to measure the frequency of each of their issues. It didn't take long for them to realize that those supervisors "downstream" of them in the process would be measuring the issues coming from them. Suddenly everyone got serious; the simple act of measuring caused people to do their jobs properly. Overnight, most of the waste went away.

The mistakes of the past now became the targets for the future. Mistakes were no longer mistakes; they were opportunities. The unofficial rework systems of the past were no longer needed; "get it right the first time" became the new credo.

This experience changed my attitude toward mistakes. I now look for them, not to punish but to practice continuous improvement. Every time I find a mistake happening at Mindshop, I look to change the process to minimize the chance of that mistake ever happening again.

Let's go back to where we started and ask again, how many mistakes do you make in a day? It doesn't matter what your answer is if you use these mistakes as an opportunity to change the process. The next stage is for you to redefine what a mistake is. It is no longer a negative but a positive. It is not a trigger for punishment but for planning. Instead of burying their mistakes, people quietly get on with changing the process. It's a complete change of culture for the organization.

Over time, the word "mistake" disappears and is replaced with the word "opportunity." The blame mentality that destroys many people and organizations dies and fades away. The workplace becomes fun and rewarding for all people at all levels. Negative people are driven from the company, which leaves positive achievers who work as a continuous-improvement team.

The resolving of "opportunities" becomes simply part of the day-to-day operation: nothing special, but what everyone does every day. You can now see that what we used to call mistakes are valuable because they are just opportunities for us to improve our processes.

What You Can Do Today—Mistakes Are Valuable

1. You can start by making a list of all the mistakes in your company. The ones you make are the easiest to spot.

2. When you get around twenty good ones, put them in order of priority and fix the best three—your best three opportunities.

3. As you resolve each set of three, select the next three, and repeat the exercise.

Chapter 11

● ● ●

What You Think You Are Is What You Get

If you have time to read only one chapter of this book, then read this one. This is the key to success in life. What does the average person think about all day? If you monitor your own thinking, you will mostly likely find that there is a significant amount of negative self-talk. You can tell what negative self-talk is because it starts with phrases like "I can't" or "It never" or even "They won't."

Another way of identifying negative self-talk is to listen to what others say. In social settings, I hear people say things like, "I am terrible at remembering names" or "I'm hopeless with money" or "I have had really bad luck finding my life partner." In a business context, I hear things like, "I've tried that before, and it didn't work" or "Our industry is different" or even "Our competitors play dirty." No matter if the negativity is blatant or subtle, the impact is the same: you get what you say.

The reason this happens is that our brains find it hard to differentiate between fact and fiction. If you walk outside and say, "It's hot," or "It's cold," your brain will believe you. Temperature is a relative thing; your body is organic, and it is your thinking that dictates how to respond to the temperature. I live in Melbourne, Australia, a city of around four million people renowned for its variation in temperature—often on the same day! The coldest place I have been so far in my life is Minneapolis, Minnesota. It was –28°C (–18°F), yet I didn't find it too cold. The hottest place I have been is my hometown of Melbourne, where it was over 45°C (113°F). I guess it's what you are used to.

It works the same with money. When I first started my consulting business in 1986, I thought every dollar was important. By the mid-1990s, I no longer worried about the dollars; I thought in thousands of dollars. By the year 2000, it was in tens of thousands, and today I'm working hard to think only in multiples of $50,000. The downside is this, however. In my early years as a consultant, I got a phone call offering me a $20,000 consulting contract, and upon hanging up, I jumped about three feet into the air with an uncharacteristic yell. To get that reaction today, it would need to be $200,000!

Practice listening to what you say and what you think. Why not record some of your conversations and analyze what you say? You will be surprised to find that there is much more negative talk than positive. The good news is, you can do something about it. As soon as you catch the thought, convert it into a positive statement. The "I always gain weight on weekends" gets turned into "I always lose weight on weekends when I walk an hour a day." The "They won't give me the order" becomes "This order is likely to be mine if I'm tenacious enough."

I use affirmations every day. My favorites are "I have an abundance of cash" and "I am being guided in everything I do." They certainly work for me; let me show you why. If I say the words "I have an abundance of cash," what do you see? If I say the words "I will never have any spare cash," now what do you see? Which would you prefer? The affirmations are not self-hypnosis; they create visions. What you see is what you get.

As you experience more success, your confidence increases. As your confidence increases, your positive self-talk increases. As your positive self-talk increases, your visions become more positive, and they become your reality.

Try it for just a day, and see and feel the difference. Even when things go wrong, the "I knew he would say no" gets converted into "This is only a temporary no, which moves me closer to the yes." Make positive thinking your new habit.

Make sure you keep your distance from people who keep feeding you negative thoughts. They are trying to bring you down to their level. Don't get sucked in. Create your own talk and your own destiny. When it is a friend who is bringing you down, change the friend. When it is a work colleague, apply for a transfer or another job. When it is a relative, try to spend less time directly in contact with the person.

This is something you can start immediately; there is nothing to get ready for. Just start changing your thinking with the very next thought. Has it worked for you? You can reinforce this approach with what you watch, what you read, and what you listen to. Read books like *You'll See It When You Believe It* by Dr. Wayne Dyer and *Grow Rich! With Peace of Mind* by Napoleon Hill; they reinforce this thinking.

What You Can Do Today—What You Think You Are Is What You Get

1. Start editing your thoughts and speech from this moment forward. Try it for an hour, and review how it went.
2. If you like this new approach, try it for four hours, then a day, then a week. Create a new way of thinking and talking. These new habits will work wonders for you. People will start noticing the difference right away.

Chapter 12

● ● ●

You Need a Point of Difference (SCA)

SCA stands for sustainable competitive advantage, your unique point of difference that makes you win on a sustainable basis. A business needs one, but so does an individual. Do you know what yours is? As I described in chapter 1, at Mindshop we call ours value to others (VTO). We put other people first.

To develop your SCA, you need to think of your options. It could be your expertise, your experience, the quality of your work, or even the way you communicate. Before I explain how to determine your SCA, let me show you how you can use it to be more strategic.

To do this, I need to assume an SCA, so I'll pick your communication skills. The SCA statement becomes: "I will win by being the best communicator in my world." Now think of all the issues you have in your life; if you could spend an hour reflecting on your issues, you would easily come up with more than a hundred. Even in a few minutes, you can think of at least ten. Here are my ten that I immediately thought of: time management, fitness, public speaking, writing skills, travel, listening skills, family, my work role next year, business growth, and fun.

What I do next is ask myself which of my ten issues would have the biggest impact on my SCA. I would pick public speaking, writing skills, and listening skills. What would you have picked? I knew mine immediately because I used another factor to help me in my decision: "the opportunity for improvement." You don't know me, so you wouldn't know which ones need the most work. When you combine the "opportunity for improvement" and "impact on the SCA," my three issues become obvious.

That's how you use an SCA, but how do you work out what yours is? Here are the steps. First, make a list of all the contenders. Although it's different for everyone, things like trust, work ethic, fun, and skills may be on your list. Aim to get twenty contenders, but don't be disappointed with only fifteen for your first attempt. We need factors that have the potential to be true sources of competitive advantage and not broad, generic factors. For example, "create significant improvement in my company's profitability" is more likely to be a sustainable competitive advantage than is "well known in the market."

At Mindshop we use three factors to help us select our own SCA. The first I call value to the customer—that is, how highly do your customers and prospects value each of your factors? Score them on a scale of one to ten, with exceptional value being a nine or ten and those of little or no importance having a low score.

The next step is simple: put a line through any factor with a score less than eight. What you have done is removed all the low-value factors to save you time. Normally you will have only three or four factors left on your list.

Now rate each of the remaining factors from one to ten on how you are currently performing on each factor (what we call current ability). This is a measure of the degree of difficulty of fixing that issue.

The last step is to score each from one to ten on how valuable it would be to fix each factor—what would the benefit be to you personally, in other words. We call this value to you.

Now all that remains is to add up the first (value to the customer) and last (value to you) scores and see which one has the highest score out of twenty. Leave out the middle score (current ability) because this is more a measure of the amount of work needed to create the specific competitive advantage. The factor with the highest score is your SCA, and you can test how it feels by putting it in an "I will win by" statement. For instance, if "work ethic" is your SCA, the statement becomes "I will win by having the best work ethic in my company." How does that feel? You can use exactly the same process to work out the SCA for a business with only a few minor changes in wording.

This SCA process is essential for you as an individual and for your business. If you have better than a hundred issues in your personal life and in your business, how do you know which issues to focus on? You only have the energy and resources to work on three issues at any one time. The average person tries to touch many issues, not doing an effective job on any. The priorities are vague and often set by others with their own agendas in mind.

By using the SCA to prioritize your issues down to just three, you will become highly focused. The focus is not driven by others; it is strategic, driven by your SCA. It doesn't mean you ignore your partner or your boss, but if you choose to put effort into the nonstrategic issues, at least you know you made the choice, and there will be internal pressures to come back to the strategic issues quickly.

What You Can Do Today—You Need a Point of Difference (SCA)

1. When you get a spare twenty minutes, list the factors for you or your business that are contenders for your SCA.
2. Score them for value to others (or value to the customer for your business).
3. Remove all factors scoring less than eight.

4. Score the remaining factors for your current competence (ability to beat competitors when doing this for your business).
5. Score them on the benefit to you (internal impact when considering your business).
6. Add the first and last score. Remember, the center column is more a measure of the degree of difficulty in fixing the SCA.
7. Test your SCA in the "I will win by" statement (or "We will win by" statement for your business).

Chapter 13

● ● ●

Respect Your Competition

What do you think about your competition? I respect mine. (Well, I respect most of my competitors.) Mindshop covers several different product areas, and if I call our business advisor support solution a product, I have three competitors that immediately come to mind, all operating internationally. None of them is in our exact space, but they all overlap to some degree.

Although I can see strategic problems with each of our competitors, I still respect them. It is not easy developing and maintaining a business in our market, and they are doing it. Their activities keep Mindshop honest, and they continuously update products, market themselves, and win new clients. I am glad they exist and survive because most of their clients aren't suitable for us. We wouldn't want them if they were offered to us. I need our competitors to survive. I'm not sure I would go out of my way to help them, but I wish them well and would not do anything to hurt them.

A representative of one of these companies contacted me a few years back because of a business magazine article in which I named his company as a competitor. He rang me to ask why I saw the company as a competitor because he didn't see Mindshop as one. I told him I agreed with him—his company was not a direct competitor—but I had nominated it as one because if you don't have an external focus on a competitor, you will end up with an internal focus and destroy yourself. I needed a competitor, and his company was the closest one I had! He liked my approach.

Respecting your competitors also means not bad-mouthing them in public or even in private, within your company. If you do, the people listening to you would be right in wondering if you bad-mouth them when they are not around. Just don't do it. Don't even think it. See the competitor as an arm's-length ally, someone you can use to focus on to continuously improve your competitive advantage.

We continuously monitor our competitors, asking people what they think of these companies, monitoring their websites, and keeping an ear open for rumors and gossip. You can find out almost anything you like with the effective use of search engines. Keep in mind that competitors will be doing the same with you, so all is fair and aboveboard. Almost twenty years ago, we did a formal review of our company versus our key competitor. We found that this company had something we needed—its UK manager! We saw her as an asset. Soon after, she began working for us, and she remains a key member of the Mindshop senior management team.

When doing your competitor review, look for gaps in the market that you can easily target. There is little value in meeting a competitor head-to-head on all fronts; you will both lose out. Look for ways to play to competitors' weaknesses and avoid their strengths.

Keep working on your product strategy. Mindshop has been known to develop new products and not use them. I like to have innovation continuously being developed. The risk is that your customers may not cope well with too much change. Over ten years ago, I invested heavily in an audiovisual package called "Win That Job." It was designed to help people get a job. It was aimed both at school dropouts and at mature workers who were facing a layoff or a career change. Until recently, it remained on the shelf—not because it is not a good product, but we just don't need it. A few weeks ago, I threw it out.

Your competitors, particularly the ones that have been around for a while, deserve respect. In terms of Mindshop's business advisor support solution, we have one impressive competitor. This company is much larger than Mindshop but is leaving huge gaps in the market that we are well placed to take advantage of. The company does a good job in a different way, and we can learn from this competitor—both in terms of things to do and things not to do.

The CEO of one of our competitors reached out this month, inviting my son James (Mindshop's managing director) and me to connect with her on LinkedIn. A few days later, she sent another message saying how impressed she was with our background, stating what a good fit we would be with her business, and asking whether we would consider becoming a customer. I assume her marketing people were driving this campaign and that she would be horrified to learn they were marketing to a competitor. The lesson from this is to focus your marketing and sales activities on people who actually need your products and services.

The competitor landscape is constantly changing, so it is essential that you continuously monitor your competitors. Competitors may not be competing with you directly, but they are still competing for the funds your customers and prospects are willing to invest. For example, our prospective accountants are deciding between investing with us and spending more money training their people in technical tax and audit skills. We accept that they need to do both and that their understanding of the tax and audit training product is superior to their understanding of the Mindshop product. Our marketing and sales process needs to educate the accountant that the future will see a demand for advisory services equal to that of both tax and audit services.

What You Can Do Today—Respect Your Competition

1. The first thing to do is a formal competitor analysis or review. Learn where you have comparative strengths, weaknesses, opportunities, and threats.
2. Never disparage your competitors publicly or privately.
3. Look at your best competitor: What should you copy, and what should you avoid?
4. Have a central file on each of your competitors that records their activities and plans.
5. Update each competitor's file on at least an annual basis.

Chapter 14

●　●　●

Be an Early Adopter

Are you a technology leader or a follower? There is a downside to both approaches. Mindshop is an early adopter: we are never the first company to do something, but we may be the second. About twenty years ago, I wrote my long-term plan for Mindshop with a focus on emerging technologies. If you watch science fiction movies like I do, you will get a glimpse of what's coming. I'm excited by virtual reality—as has been mentioned in several chapters of this book—but we won't be the first consulting group, training organization, or professional services firm to use the technology when it gets released. Nonetheless, we have recently launched a chat-bot called Ask Mindshop, a key first step.

I was the same when data projectors were released. We persevered with overhead projectors for a couple more years until the size and price of the projectors came down. By waiting, we were better placed to afford the technology and to understand how best to use it. We did the same with videoconferencing. We played with it for years until broadband became global, and then we moved. The added benefit was the additional features that got bundled in with the videoconference product: built-in whiteboards, the ability to control desktops, and recording the sessions for streaming on the web.

If you become an early adopter of technology, you will attract others interested in emerging technology. The people attracted to you will be in four important groups: customers, suppliers, strategic alliances, and employees. The research says that early adopters are about 13 percent of the population, so it's not a big group. They tend to hang out in the same places; find a few, and you'll find more. You need to be one yourself to find them.

A note of caution: you should not be too innovative and therefore risk a disconnection with others—specifically, your customers and colleagues. That doesn't mean you cannot take risks, however. I was asked to run a Mindshop tools session for some eight-year-old students at a progressive private school. I promised to be able to solve any problem they wanted. The problem they wanted me to solve was to fly, and they didn't mean in an aircraft.

I got them to close their eyes and imagine they were outside on the grass with their arms outstretched like an airplane. (By the way, about ten adults were also in the group following the same instructions.) I then asked the children to start running, fast, and immediately the room was filled with the sound of little feet running in place. As a result, the children imagined they had been flying, and the adults just sat there wondering what had happened. The children appreciated the innovation, but I was not sure what the adults thought, except for the school principal, who commented at the end of the session that it was the best example of creative visualization he had ever seen.

Most emerging technology brings with it such benefits as improved efficiencies. Videoconferencing brings with it improved communication, lower travel costs, and enhanced relationships. The "soft" benefits like enhanced relationships are just as important as the "hard" benefits like lower travel costs.

To ensure that I find the right emerging technologies, I invest time in searching the Internet for sites on the latest computer innovations, mobile devices, business and personal improvement tools, and current thought-leadership events. I spend time in online bookshops looking at the new books being released. I focus on nonfiction books, but I do wonder if I should be looking at fiction as well. I prefer e-books and audiobooks, as I like to have them all on my mobile devices.

I like science fiction. The technologies in *Star Wars*–type movies are now finding their way into our everyday lives, particularly in the areas of communication and entertainment. There is a reason for this. People buy emotion. A movie is usually packaged emotion. So is a videophone conference with your spouse or a close friend. People will pay for this, so these solutions come out first. Once the costs become even reasonably affordable, the technologies can be adapted for business use.

What do you think is coming next? What should you be researching? My great hope is in virtual reality, augmented reality, machine learning, and artificial intelligence. I have been investigating these technologies for twenty-plus years. I read everything I can on virtual reality. I'm in the business of giving advice and coaching support. When I started doing this type of work thirty years ago, my technology was a rudimentary computer, an electronic typewriter, and a mobile phone installed in my car. In those days, I used to drive vast distances, and the greatest value I provided to my clients was in face-to-face meetings and workshops. When I get virtual reality as a medium, the value will become my intellectual property; I will no longer need to be physically present. My ability to solve problems and drive change will be leveraged. This will further open up the world as my market, and at the same time, costs will continue to come down so that more people will be able to afford me.

In the meantime, I am patiently using the current technologies such as the Internet, multimedia, videoconferencing, and web conferencing. These technologies are fantastic, particularly when compared to thirty years ago. Just imagine what it will be like in ten years' time! The difference is that I won't be physically there; it will be an avatar providing business advice, a computer-generated person that looks, sounds, and thinks like me.

There is a part of my job that the avatar won't be able to do, of course, and that's building relationships and trust with key clients. With the advent of virtual reality, I will have more time for self-education and research and cultivating those relationships. I can't think of anything better to do; I am excited about working for several more decades.

How will virtual reality change your industry and your job? Does the prospect excite you as it does me? I developed my vision of Mindshop for forty-two years' time, worked out where I was on that day, and developed a plan of how to steadily work toward my vision. I feel I am waiting for technology to catch up with my vision, but because I am enjoying the journey, there is no rush.

What You Can Do Today—Be an Early Adopter

1. Look at what technology is emerging around you, and review how effectively you are adapting and utilizing it to make your life more efficient and more valuable to your customers.
2. Read everything you can about those emerging technologies.

Chapter 15

●　●　●

Core Values Drive Everything

Where do your core values come from? Were you born with them, or did you learn them? Psychologists believe you are largely formed by the age of seven, so most of your core values will also be in place by then. You can adjust your values as you grow and learn, but your parents or primary caregivers are the major factor in the formation of your values.

Your business also has core values. They are also largely formed by the time your business is seven years old, and the "parents" of the business are the major factor in the formation of the organizational values. The parents are the founders and directors, but all the members of the team have an impact on values. Organizations fall apart if the core values are corrupt or there is conflict in the values.

How do you determine the core values of an organization? We do it by asking two simple questions. The first question is, "What is important to you about working at...?" When answering this question for Mindshop, answers like fun, growth, integrity, and trust come to mind. The second question is, "What has to happen for you to know that you have...?" For me, that becomes, "What has to happen for you to know you have integrity or trust or growth?" The answers drill down to things like community contribution, value to others, and continuous improvement.

We set the five core values a long time ago, and they have not changed because they still work for us. The five core values we focus on are these: value to others, best practice, continuous improvement, community contribution, and fun. Value to others means putting the other person's needs first. Best practice comes from other industries, so you need to work across all types of businesses. Continuous improvement means improving the processes in your organization in all ways and involving all the people. Community contribution reminds us that we need to invest in the communities that we live and work in. Fun means just what it says—namely, having fun every day in the business.

Your core values help you make decisions. Just make sure you do not fall into the trap of having too many. Five is about the right number. We run a lot of conferences for our community of advisors and business leaders globally. When designing the program, selecting speakers, and deciding on venues, we test our options against the five core values. We have to score well on all five. We can't leave any of the core values out.

Another critical business activity where core values are important is recruiting new people, both new customers and new staff members. Consider your values as the ticket to doing business with you, the ticket to the game. Your questions need to test the fit of the person with your core values. You also need to keep the core values at the top of your mind when solving problems. You may have a performance issue with a staff member. By applying the core values, you know what to do. With a Mindshop staff member, we need to make sure the outcome is of value to the individual, it is best practice, it will contribute to the improvement of our processes, it helps the "community," and it's fun. Although these five core values do not impact equally on the situation under review, it is essential to consider each of them.

At Mindshop there have been situations where the value to others (VTO) core value has been broken. For me that is unacceptable, and unless it was just an accident, it will result in removal from Mindshop. Conflict in the core values is like cancer in the body; it needs to be dealt with quickly and removed completely.

We had a situation where a person was perceived to have breached the VTO core value; the pressure mounted to remove that person from the network, and we did. Several years later, this person contacted me and put forth the case that he had been wrongly accused and that he deserved to be allowed back. I wasn't sure where the truth lay, so I agreed he could come back. I gave him the benefit of the doubt because it was a value to him. The outcome was that he reverted to his previous behavior, and he was removed for a second time and will not be allowed back.

On reflection, this was the right thing to do, and the right outcome resulted. Even though I have a PhD in psychology, I am not sure why this person is like he is, but it is my job to select the core values and also my job to help police them.

Another example was at a Mindshop weekend retreat, which we ran very early in our development. The theme of the conference was vision. We rented a resort on a lake, invited the families of our staff members, and made sure we had some fun time included in the program. To reinforce the vision and to tap the core values of best practice, fun, and even VTO, we arranged for a team to take up any of the group who wanted to go on a hang glider that was towed by a boat on the lake to a height of several hundred feet and then cut free to fly back to the start point. A qualified and experienced pilot was in tandem with each person. It certainly made an impact with most of the adults who chose to fly. Everything looked different from that height. The need for understanding where you are, where you want to be, and how to get there safely was reinforced indelibly.

What You Can Do Today—Core Values Drive Everything

1. Apply the two questions, "What is important to you about working at...?" and "What has to happen for you to know that you have...?" so that you can identify your core values.
2. Think about everywhere in your life the core values apply. Where is there a good fit, and where is there conflict?
3. Publish your core values for all to see.
4. Memorize them. If you have to look them up, you don't believe in them.

Chapter 16

●　●　●

Community Contribution

Community contribution is one of the five core values of Mindshop. It is also a major plank of our strategy. When Mindshop was founded, we set up a charity and strongly encouraged all the members of our global network to provide their time free of charge to help us with the charitable work. Most did and still do, and so as Mindshop has grown, so has the charity.

The Mindshop Educational Trust, as the charity is called, runs one-week structured work-experience programs for fifteen- to sixteen-year-old students. On the first day, a Mindshop advisor trains the group of around five or six students in use of the core Mindshop tools; for the next four days, they act as consultants to a host company such as Toyota, AMCOR, a manufacturing company, an accounting firm, or even Mindshop itself.

The following three days requires them to work out where their project is now, where they need it to be in the future, and then how to implement the plan to achieve the solution to their problem or opportunity. On the final day, the students formally present their findings and recommendations to the senior management team of the host company, always surprising them with their innovation and astute insights. Also present will be representatives of their school and their parents. This is a daunting situation for young people, but they always do a good job, in part because they generally have a "can-do" attitude. When you couple this with the Mindshop tools and processes, the result is an outstanding win-win outcome. I run several programs each year myself, and it is very rewarding for me personally.

If I bring someone into the Mindshop network and show her how to be more successful, but she doesn't feel worthy of this new success, she will end up sabotaging herself and blaming me for her misfortune. I had to build a self-worth mechanism into the Mindshop business model to minimize this possibility—hence, the Mindshop Educational Trust.

You don't need to have your own charity to enable the self-worth mechanism, but it helps! If you belong to a service club such as Rotary or Lions or you coach or manage your children's soccer or basketball team, you are already doing it. The key is to give back to the community that indirectly feeds you.

I am proud to see the Mindshop Excellence groups forming all over the world in each of the countries we operate in. When I extrapolate this process out ten or twenty years, I get excited to think of the good we will be providing. Already I get letters from students who participated in a Mindshop Educational Trust group years earlier telling me what an impact it had on them.

My wife, Julie, manages the day-to-day operation of the Mindshop Educational Trust, and the personal growth she has received from it is in direct proportion to the energy she invests in her charitable work. Other staff members are also involved, and several teachers and Mindshop advisors also participate on the trust's board.

I am not surprised to see the people who run several programs a year doing so well in their business and personal lives in spite of the huge time commitment they invest in facilitating Mindshop Excellence programs in their cities. We don't push people to get involved, but it is the perfect opportunity to practice your Mindshop tools and processes with a challenging audience.

Young people get bored quickly; if they can't see the relevance of what they are being taught, they will say so. They don't automatically accept everything you say; if it doesn't make sense, they will need a more detailed explanation. This forces you to think deeply about the "why" of both the "what" and the "how" you are providing them with.

Another benefit of putting back into your community is that it keeps your feet on the ground. In business, as you rise up the food chain, your exposure to "real" people becomes less and less. Getting involved in community activities grounds you. I remember doing a course in London with some health workers. They didn't care if I was the president of a company and an ex-CEO of an international public company. They gave me no recognition for my experience or qualifications; they judged me only on what they saw then and there.

I realized that I had developed a habit of bullying people with my seniority, and this time they were having none of it. Fortunately, I reflected after a day of being ignored based on my style and made the changes to my approach that made me a little more acceptable on day two of the training. I continue to look for opportunities to dress down my style and merge into the crowd. I talk to people on planes, on buses, and at the local coffee shop. I like shopping with my wife in the local supermarket, content with just pushing the cart. Community is what makes life meaningful. Recognize the benefits you get from your community, and balance the ledger by putting back even more than you get.

What You Can Do Today–Community Contribution

1. The starting point is to take stock of how much you have put back into your community over the past year. Be honest with yourself, and think about how you can lift your game.

2. What can you do to give back? Start small, and build up your level of contribution.

3. If you are a member of Mindshop, talk to us about running a Mindshop Excellence program where you went to school or where your children go to school. We have an information packet we can send to you, but most of the information is available on the Mindshop website.

Chapter 17

● ● ●

Maintaining Life Balance

I believe there are six key areas in your life, and they don't include work. Work is the vehicle we use to achieve the six life-balance areas of family, finances, health, mental development, philosophy/belief system, and social life. Before I explain each of these, let's look at how we use this model. We all invest different levels of energy in the various elements of our lives. The tendency for many people is to invest most of their energy in one or two areas and ignore one or two of the rest. This results in an unbalanced life. By managing each area of your life, you can become balanced, much like a wheel.

If we take social life, I can demonstrate what I mean. I'll assume you are in your midthirties and have a couple of children. What is your social life like? Does it just evolve, or are you managing it? Whom do you socialize with—mostly people from work or family members? If you had a magic wand and could create the ideal social life for you, what would it look like? Now measure yourself against the magic-wand version of your social life: Where do you need to make changes?

Another area is health. How much energy do you spend in this area? What could you do to improve your health? Are you spending too much time in this sector (some people do)? What can you do to improve your health like you did your social life?

Now for finance. Most people want to do better financially. My philosophy used to be to spend my money and save what was left. The trouble with this approach was that there was never any money left, so I made a subtle change. I now save my money and spend what's left. See the difference? Can you do a better job of managing your finances, and if so, how will you do it? The issue of spending too much time in this sector may apply to some of you.

The next factor is family. How well are you doing? How much time do you spend each week one-on-one with each of your children? If you don't have children, how much time do you spend each week one-on-one with your parents? The average father spends less than ten minutes a week in true one-on-one activities. Sitting on the couch watching football together does not count; you have to talk to one another. What can you do to improve your performance?

Mental development is an interesting factor. While we are enrolled in formal education, our rate of learning peaks. For many, however, once they finish their schooling, the rate of learning slows. My favorite saying is, slightly adapted from the words of a former boss mentioned in chapter 3, "If a person believes his or her education is finished, then that person is finished." What books do you read? What documentaries do you watch? What courses are you taking? Can you improve your mental development, and if so, how?

The final factor is philosophy; it can also mean religion. It's what you believe in. How much time and energy do you invest in working on your philosophy? This could involve the books you read, the groups you belong to, and/or the websites you look at. What can you do to improve your performance in philosophy?

With so many things to fix, let me show you how to fast-track your development. This week I read two books: one on spiritual matters and the other on quantum physics. In doing so, I contributed to the mental and philosophy categories at the same time. I mix social and family all the time, as I'm sure you do. My rule of thumb when inviting someone to join the Mindshop community is to ask myself, "Could I ask this person home for dinner?" I don't want to spend all the time I do working if I don't enjoy the company of the people I work with.

As I mentioned earlier (and have now confirmed), work is the vehicle you use to get finance, mental, and all the other life-balance factors in shape. I love my work because it provides me with more than money. Do you love your work? Is it providing you with everything you need? What changes do you need to make? Score each of the six life-balance areas as to your current level of satisfaction in each; then think about what your target scores should be. Where are the gaps? Any gaps will mean your wheel of life will not turn smoothly. What action plans will enable you to close those gaps? You do not need a perfect score in each of the ten factors; it is more important to make sure your wheel is balanced.

What You Can Do Today—Maintaining Life Balance

1. Review the six life-balance areas, score where you are now and where you want to be, and make sure your targets are balanced. You don't need scores of ten; it's about balance.
2. Determine how you will close any gaps.
3. Look for opportunities to resolve two or more areas with one action plan. The key is to balance your life.

Chapter 18

● ● ●

Relationship Selling

Think about what you sell and why people buy it. Are they buying from you or your organization? You should find that they are buying from you because, to them, you are the organization. If you accept that they are buying from you, then ask yourself why. What is the main reason they buy from you? Some of you may answer, "Because it's easier to buy from me than someone else," or "Because we have the best price." The majority of you will answer, "Because they trust me."

Now that raises some interesting points. Why do they trust you? Would they still buy from you if a competitor offered them similar goods and services at a lower price? How much lower would the price need to be to trigger a mass exodus of customers? What sits behind all these questions is the fact that you have a relationship with them, and your competitors probably don't.

They know you, warts and all, and deep down, they know that the competitor may look good on the surface, but will it have faults they can't see? If this logic is right—and I believe it is—then your relationship with your customers is part of your competitive edge. How did you get this relationship? How has it changed over time? Does it always get better as time goes on? If you had your time over again with each customer, could you do a better job of building a relationship with the customer?

As with any relationship, it is, at any specific point in time, the sum total of all the experiences that they and you have been through together. If these experiences are mostly positive, then you have an excellent relationship; if they are mostly negative, then you have a poor relationship. If you want to change a bad relationship into a good one, all you need to do is to have more positive experiences.

Think about all your customers, both internal and external. Rate each relationship, with zero being very poor and ten being very good. Think about how much effort you would need to invest to get every relationship to a good level. Do you want to do this with each of them? Do you have the time and energy required to do so? If not, then how many on the customer list could you handle?

What are you thinking? Are you excited or depressed? You will probably find that with some customers, it would take too much effort to fix the relationship. You may find that you are investing too much energy in relationships that are already good. What I suggest is that you decide which customers are too much trouble; have a list of them so that you constantly remind yourself that these people are earmarked for the wastebasket. Work out which customers you are investing too much time in. You have theoretically now freed up a large part of your time and energy, probably as much as 50 percent of your customer contact time. Where would you like to invest it?

Go to the next group from the top of your list; these will be the customers you should spend more time with in order to build a relationship. Allocate your spare energy to as many as you can. Develop a specific one-page plan for each. You can select from a variety of relationship-building activities to make sure you improve your performance with this group. Your starting point is a contact program, followed by phone calls, e-mails, letters, social media connections, meetings, and even invitations to social events. Make sure you create positive experiences with each. Make sure every link to these customers does what it is supposed to. Deliver to them on time, on specification, and at the right price. You need to make dealing with you both professional and fun.

Look at your time spent working. How much time do you spend in relationship building? I consider that almost all of my time is spent doing this with both customers and prospects. I try to make every contact I have with these important people fun and different so that I stand out. Around 90 percent of the people I meet love it; the other 10 percent don't like it. This is because I am being myself. I don't try to work out what people want me to be and change my style accordingly. Being yourself is like always telling the truth; it is much easier to do than trying to be someone else.

If you don't have good chemistry with someone, accept it and move on. There are billions of other people in the world you can relate to; talk to them. Build trust and understanding with others. Ask them questions about themselves without being selfish about sharing information about yourself. Your aim is to get the other person talking, so practice asking good questions. Questions that generate yes and no answers are not normally good questions.

Take responsibility for a relationship. Don't keep score, thinking to yourself, "I contacted him last time, so now it's up to him!" A relationship is a two-way street, but it is not a 50:50 deal when it comes to who does what. There is always one of you doing a little bit more in the relationship—or even a lot more. If you value the relationship, there is nothing wrong with taking the lead in terms of keeping the relationship going.

What You Can Do Today—Relationship Selling

1. Start by making a list of people in your life, both business and personal relationships, whom you would like to put in the wastebasket. Work out plans on how to do that.

2. Determine which people you spend too much time on, and work out how to wind them back a notch or two. What you have left is a prioritized list of people you need to build better relationships with.
3. Develop a plan for each of the key ones. The plan should include activities, such as a contact program; how to be of high value to them; and if it's a business relationship, how you will sell them more or serve them better.

Chapter 19

● ● ●

Reinventing Yourself

Do you have an exit strategy for your current job? If not, you need one! If you are a baby boomer, then it may be an exit plan to retire in ten years. If you belong to Generation Y, then it may be a plan for your next career move in two years' time. If you are moving on, who will do your job? It was back in the seventies when my career started to take off. In the first decade, I changed jobs with little thought about what I was leaving behind. On reflection, that was not right. I cared for my employers, my coworkers, and my internal and external customers, yet I just walked out on them to the next job with little thought or care about what happened to them.

All that changed in the eighties, when I started to think about leaving a legacy. I thought about my next move and how I would transition my leadership to the next person. In 1986, when I left Laser Lab, I gave more than three months' notice. My boss, the chairman of the group, didn't speak to me from the day I resigned, but no matter. I had a big order in the wings in China. I knew if I left, the Chinese would not buy, so I decided to stay until the order came through. I wrote to the Chinese customer, explaining that I was leaving and starting my own business; it was essential that I got the customer's order in August.

The Chinese wrote back, saying to come in August but that they wouldn't have the approval to sign a contract by then. I was to come anyway, for they wanted to negotiate with me, and if we reached an agreement, they would let me sign the contract, go home, and start my business. And then, when they could, they would send me the signed contract. I flew out, spent three weeks negotiating, had a delightful signing ceremony where only I signed, and then flew back to Australia with my copy of the contract. My boss was not impressed (so I heard). A contract with only one signature on it was worthless in his mind. I kept working until, many weeks later, the letter of credit was in place, and only then did I pack my desk and go off to start my own business.

I didn't feel I could put any effort into my new business until I had the transition from Laser Lab right. I left on a Friday, and on the following Monday, I sat at my kitchen table and thought, "Now I will set up Chris Mason & Associates." I know—it was a terrible name, but that's what I did, and Julie and I effectively started the precursor to Mindshop on August 11, 1986.

I had made sure there was a succession plan at Laser Lab covering the leadership, the staff, the customers, and the company, even if no one else cared. In my own business, it was even easier. I knew that to protect my family, I needed a succession plan. In the early days, it was just Julie, me, and some subcontractors; my succession plan was a key-man insurance policy so that if I died, Julie had money to reestablish her life. That policy is still in place today.

As Mindshop grew, I kept identifying my next job in the growth phase and developing someone to take my place. Here I learned an important lesson. People can look to have all the attributes needed to take over, but until you try it, you don't know if it will work. I had three failed attempts at a successor for me. Mostly they were good people; they just weren't the right fit for this particular job. It was a difficult role—strategist, speaker, supervisor, and product developer.

It wasn't until I put my son James into the role that it worked for me. James had grown up with the business, having been nine years old when we founded it. He earned a computer science degree at a local university and started working part-time with us while he was studying. Once his degree was completed, he came on board full-time to develop our IT infrastructure, a key role in the Mindshop current and future strategy.

Julie and I were in London when a serious situation arose back in Australia that involved embezzlement of company funds at Mindshop. I saw an opportunity. I gave James the job of sorting out the fraud, even though he was only twenty-two years old. I estimated that the total cost to Mindshop was around $400,000, considering all the direct and hidden costs. But I figured if I had "invested" this much money, I should get a return on it. It was worth the investment if it levered James into the top role and gave him a fast track to managing director.

The fraud was a distraction to others in and around Mindshop, so no one complained to me about having such a young person in charge. James rose to the occasion and did a fantastic job sorting out the mess and getting the business back to a sound and profitable state. My succession plan had started, and my time was freed up to focus on building the international market for Mindshop.

The lesson I learned from this is that you need to test your succession plan. Putting James in charge while I was still operational in the business was a good insurance policy. I was there to coach and support and even jump back in if needed. (I plan to work another fifteen years or more, so I can still be part of James's succession plan in an emergency.) We then invited my daughter, Emily, into the business, which further strengthened the succession plan.

I handed over my role as sole leader long ago, but I have retained other roles, such as a coach and developer of intellectual property for the business. The Mindshop business model addresses this succession need. We are continuously training and developing the people in the network. Some of the advisors stand out because of their core values, their success using Mindshop in their businesses, and the respect they have gained from other members of the Mindshop community. As we need more coaches, we just hire these people on a contract basis. The scalability of this model will ensure we have sufficient coaches to enable and maintain our current strong growth trend, and—importantly—each one has the same core values as we do.

What You Can Do Today–Reinventing Yourself

1. Make a list of all your core duties.
2. Work out how you can develop a person or persons to replace you in each role.
3. Test your plan by giving these people tasks while you are still around. By using the same approach for all your key people, succession will never be an issue, ensuring ongoing customer and shareholder value.

Chapter 20

● ● ●

Focus on Customer Lifetime Value

Wat are your customers worth to you? I use the customer lifetime value (CLV) rule to work it out for Mindshop. I estimate that the average Mindshop advisor spends around $10,000 (that's Australian dollars) a year with us and stays an average of ten years. This means that, on average, every time an advisor agrees to join Mindshop, it has a CLV of $100,000. How much effort would you go to for a $100,000 sale?

If an organization agrees to ten licenses, I regard it as a $1 million sale, and I find that very exciting. If you can see my logic of CLV, then it will change your thinking in some key areas of your business. What sales process do you need for a million-dollar sale? Who would be capable of negotiating a million-dollar deal? How long does it take to get someone to agree to a million-dollar sale? What due diligence would that person need to do for it? What paperwork is appropriate for such a deal?

The level of professionalism needs to lift significantly. Applying the CLV rule to your business, what changes would you need to make? Let's take two examples: the first is an advisory business, and the second is a manufacturing organization. Both will need to make strategic changes due to the CLV rule.

All the questions regarding sales process, salesperson, timing, due diligence, and paperwork still apply in both cases.

Assume you are a business advisor. Your average customer gives you an engagement worth $10,000, and he or she engages you several times over a three-year period. At that point, something happens, and that customer moves on. You need to be continuously hunting and gathering to find new clients. I hated these boom-and-bust cycles when I was consulting. The bottom line is that your CLV is around $30,000.

What would you have to do to get the average engagement to, say, $20,000? It is a 100 percent increase, but it is not difficult. What if I convinced the client to go to a $2,000-a-month retainer, and I bundled in a strategic planning front end and ongoing coaching and support for project teams and focused on growing the client's business by 20 percent each year (and increasing the client's profit at the same level)? The retainer means we now have an annual sale of $24,000, but what other needs—clearly outside the scope of the retainer—would you identify along the way? Assume you and the client identify three projects worth $10,000 for each year. You have increased the annual fees from this client to $54,000!

To do this will mean you have to change. Relationships will need to develop, your skills and confidence will need to grow, you will need to be able to refocus on new issues/opportunities each year, and your ability to manage projects must be very good. In doing this, assume you are able to retain the client for ten years; your CLV is now $540,000! Isn't that exciting? How many clients do you now need to earn a fair return for your skills and experience? What if you had three and, say, another ten under development? What a great business you now have!

Now let's take the second example: the manufacturing organization. We'll assume the average order quantity is $1,000, the client orders once a month, and the client stays around for five years—a CLV of $60,000. So, to up the CLV, you focus on the variables of average sale value (or purchasing additional products/services), frequency of orders, and length of time as a customer, but despite all your best efforts in these areas, this client can only be developed to a CLV of $100,000. The next variable you need to target is your total number of customers. What if we could increase it from ten to one hundred? The point is that in some businesses the CLV is not endless; there are levels that would require investment and resources beyond which you are comfortable. We all have choices, and a key choice is to choose your business model.

Fewer customers but with a high CLV is good for some, but losing even one customer can cause significant cash-flow problems. More customers with a lower CLV will require different systems and is a lower risk to your cash flow, but sometimes it takes just as much time and energy to win a low-CLV customer as it does a high-CLV customer.

I do think about CLV, but I am holding the average sale per year constant and working on extending the number of years that clients stay with us by continuously innovating and improving our offering and value for money. I would like to find that the average length of time clients stay with Mindshop is twenty years. That would increase my CLV to $200,000. I believe that is where we are now, but I need to prove it before I "officially" change the CLV. My next challenge would then be how to increase the average years with us to forty. How good would that be? In effect, a cradle-to-grave support solution!

Your challenge is to determine your variables and your CLV and then to develop specific plans to double the CLV, then double it again, and then again. It will force you to fix issues like product range, on-time delivery, customer relationships, customer quality, technology utilization, attraction and retention of staff, continuous improvement, innovation, and pricing.

What You Can Do Today—Focus on Customer Lifetime Value

1. Work out your CLV as it is today by calculating the average annual sale per customer and multiplying it by the number of years you retain your customers.
2. Develop a plan to double the CLV. What needs to change? You will find issues in your sales process, your own skills/capabilities, your customer contact program, your product range, and customer quality.
3. Make the changes, and remeasure the CLV. Once the CLV doubles, develop a plan to double it again. The CLV amount should become a lifetime quest for you.

Chapter 21

●　●　●

The Trust Equation

I am a very trusting person; it's the way my mother brought me up. I can't change because I don't want to change. People have taken advantage of my trust throughout my life, but that's a small price to pay to retain my trust in others. As my trust has been broken, I have changed people and systems to minimize the probability of that incident happening again.

The adage that you should trust people until they break that trust is how most people think. When you are driving a car, you trust the other drivers to stay on their side of the road. You know that occasionally people do make a mistake and drive on the wrong side of the road and cause accidents, but that doesn't stop you from driving. The probability is that this year, every time you drive, all the drivers around you will stay on their side of the road, and you won't have an accident.

It comes down to probability. You can manage this probability. If you leave a $100 note on the family dining table, what's the probability it will still be there tomorrow? In my family, it is certain to still be there. What is the probability that if you left $100 on a seat at the airport, someone would hand it in? I think it is better than 50 percent, although I have never tested it.

Where do we trust people at work? We trust them in the areas of honesty, customer care, working hours, loyalty, safety, and obedience. Can we trust each person to the same degree in all of these areas? Are all individuals equally trustworthy? The answer is no. Should we develop our systems for the lowest common denominator or the highest? As with driving, we look at the consequences of a breach of trust and develop the system accordingly. That's why they install crash barriers on some bends on major highways and not on the straightaways; there is a greater probability of another driver coming onto your side of the road while turning into the bend.

In a business situation, the same logic applies. Where do you need crash barriers in your business? At Mindshop we don't leave a lot of cash in the office. We lock our office when we go home at night. I have a complex password to enter my secure coaching area on the Mindshop website. I'm sure you do these sorts of things as well. So does that mean we are trusting or not trusting? I suggest we are trusting of others, but we don't want to leave temptation in others' way.

We need to look at people in two ways: based on their enthusiasm and their skill levels. If a person is low in enthusiasm and high in skills, she needs motivation. If a person is low in enthusiasm and low in skills, she needs supervision. If she is high in enthusiasm and low in skills, she needs instruction. And, finally, if she is high in enthusiasm and high in skills, she needs to be trusted.

What if you have someone who is high in enthusiasm and high in skills, and you trust him, and he breaks your trust? The answer is, it depends on the issue. If it is a core value issue, like stealing from you, the answer is to dismiss him immediately. If the issue is not as serious—say he didn't follow up with a customer as he had promised to do—you need to counsel him. There is another overlapping factor here: it also depends on who the person is. If she is family, you will have almost endless patience. If she is a customer, then dropping the account should happen more quickly. With a member of your staff, it will be somewhere in between.

Every case will be different, but the bottom line is that your aim is to trust as many people as possible. Imagine what life would be like if you could trust everyone. Don't despair: the good news is that you can trust most people, but it all depends on the circumstances. The starting point is you. Can you be trusted? Your ability to trust others is directly linked to how much you trust yourself.

I once had someone tell me I am too trusting. At the time, I thought two things: what a compliment, and what does that tell me about that person? My immediate response was: "Thank you. I won't change, as it was the way I was brought up." If this person had said that I needed better systems to avoid having my trust broken in the future, my answer would have been, "I agree. Any ideas how we do that?"

What You Can Do Today—The Trust Equation

1. The starting point is to think of the probability and consequences of having your trust broken in a variety of situations. Can people steal from you? Will people do what they say?
2. The next step is to build backup plans and systems to minimize the temptation for people to not be trustworthy. These are just common-sense things you should do. The bottom line is that when you are in a position where you are not sure whether to trust someone, give that person the benefit of the doubt and trust him or her. You'll be pleasantly surprised 99 percent of the time.

Chapter 22

●　●　●

Build Value Reserves

Where do you store value? Most people answer by saying "in the bank and in my home." We are all as rich today as the kings were in the Middle Ages. We have more luxury, more comfort, and more safety. I think we all want to see this continue, and we don't compare ourselves with kings in the Middle Ages—we compare ourselves with our neighbors, friends, and peers.

I want to bring in another factor: goodwill. On an accounting balance sheet, you will often see goodwill as an asset. The same applies to our lives, but for now, let's look at where you have goodwill stored in your business. The first place people think of is the company's brand. Mindshop is a brand. Most people think well of the brand; it stands for best practice, professionalism, and value for money. I also have a brand. I stand for professionalism, integrity, innovation, and fun. That doesn't mean I am perfect in each area, however; we all make mistakes. It means, this is what I want to be known for, and I work hard at being good at each factor.

You can build value reserves in your house, your retirement fund, and your investments, but all they do is provide financial security. Money does not make you happy, but it can make you unhappy if you don't have enough. Money can provide you with opportunities, but, again, it does not guarantee happiness. So how much is enough? I know for myself that I can live quite frugally now: my children are educated, and I have no debt personally or in the business. I have always liked the thought that you should have cash reserves equal to one year's operating expenses, both personally and in your business.

You can also build value reserves in your relationships with people. For example, if I asked all my customers for more business from them and referrals to their friends, I could probably double the size of my business very quickly. I don't do that because we are already growing well each year, and I have as my first priority making sure we provide good value to current customers (and have fun in the journey). I strongly believe that life is not about the destination; it is all about the journey, and I am in no rush.

I like the fact that I have stored value in my customer base. My aim is to build even more stored value because it is the key factor in our having a new business pipeline that generates high annual growth. A strong growth rate of 20 percent each year for ten years would make us around six times the size we are today. How many customers will we have then, and what stored value will be in the client list?

You also store value in your team members. We have a number of team members with more than twenty years of service with us. They know how to do their respective jobs, but they also know the history of Mindshop and most of our Mindshop community. How much value would you put on this knowledge? There is a way you can maximize this value; training your people in multiple skills to equip them to play a variety of roles and to increase their value to the company is an obvious way.

Above all, I wanted to take a more revolutionary approach. About ten years ago, I saw that the knowledge stored in Mindshop—and in me personally—was a huge asset. It will be the same for you and your organization as well. I observed in other companies that people retired or died, and their knowledge went with them. Little, if any, effort was put into capturing this information before they left. I looked at what information would be lost if I died unexpectedly, and I decided to make videos of all the important things I knew.

The Mindshop toolbox was created in written and video form in the late nineties. I recorded around fifty videos, initially in a professional studio and then in our own training room. Around the same time, we established a knowledge database where our thought-leadership papers, business tools, and even experiences could be stored and viewed by all, and people were encouraged to contribute their knowledge to it.

Over the years—and now decades later—we have significantly improved the toolbox: the videos are now online, the contributions from the Mindshop community are increasing, and it is no longer just about what I know and think. These Mindshop databases and the nearly one thousand people on our platform are now our stored value.

Another area where we store value is with our alliance partners. We know we can't reach everyone we want to directly, so we align ourselves with people who have an existing relationship with those people we are targeting. We have alliances with many of the middle-tier accounting networks. We give to them before we receive. That's how relationships are formed: by exchanging value.

The most valued part of our stored value is our future plans. They are so valuable that I won't be mentioning them in this book. I don't think any competitor could utilize the plans, but you never know. These jewels in our stored-value vault will remain under lock and key until we need them.

What You Can Do Today—Build Value Reserves

1. Make a list of all the places where you have value stored. This chapter has listed a lot of places where you can store value reserves, with the

bank balance and goodwill being the ones that show on your company's balance sheet. Other places include the untouched sales in your customer list, the knowledge of your staff, your databases, and your intellectual property.

2. Estimate what they are worth to you today.
3. Develop one action to continuously increase the stored value in each area on your list.

Chapter 23

● ● ●

Look at Other Industries for Best Practice

Are you applying best practice? Do you know best practice comes from industries other than your own? Retailers are usually best at customer service. Automotive component manufacturers are usually best at waste reduction (efficiency). What are you good at? Is it the world's best practice? Why not?

Many people work hard to build the top line in their businesses: the sales. Why push more business through an incapable system? Profit is the reward for your investment of time and money in your business. Your aim should be to execute "best practice" to improve your profit and then to boost your sales.

The key is to study what others are doing and learn from them. You can do this by keeping your eyes open when shopping. Even at your local shopping center, there are lessons to learn. Copy things that you observe and think are good. Make sure you don't copy things you observe and think are bad.

What things do you like about your local supermarkets? I like that they position products so that they are convenient to buy. I like the variety. I like that they can be a one-stop shop: I can buy bread, milk, and fruit, as well as wheel cleaner for my car. What things can you learn from your favorite restaurant? I like the friendly and knowledgeable service, the atmosphere created by the layout, and the chance to try things I don't normally have at home.

Which are the best supermarket and the best restaurant you have ever experienced? Why did they stand out? What lessons did you learn from them? My best supermarket was open twenty-four hours, with wide aisles and bright lighting. My best restaurant (a French restaurant in London) had lots of courses, all of which were very small portions of a wide variety of food, and an excellent wine list.

Think about your business. Which areas are the most important to your customers? If it is customer service, think about the lessons from the supermarket and the restaurant. Can you use any of these ideas? Now think about the leader in your market: What is this company doing that is making it the leader? If it is marketing, then which company exemplifies the world's best practice in marketing? Is it Microsoft? Is it Qantas? Is it Apple? It doesn't matter which company you pick—we all will see it differently—but what is this company doing that you can do?

Spend time thinking about what you could do differently. Maybe you can't have twenty television advertisements running each day, but you can have an informative and interactive website. As technology advances, you can compete toe-to-toe with the big guys. Your website can be just as good as those of Microsoft, Qantas, or Apple.

Now think about what you need. If it is profit, then which company exemplifies best practice in creating profit? The next question to ask yourself is this: Is it the total amount of profit, or is it the percentage of sales? I don't see Mindshop rivaling Microsoft in annual sales, but can we make more profit on every dollar we do create? I love profit because when your price point is competitive, if you are making a profit, it means you are efficient and probably have good customer service due to the lower waste in your business. If waste removal (efficiency) is the thing you need, then think about the companies that are the best in the world at that. I believe it is the automotive component manufacturers. They have few customers, who set the prices at global best practice. They have no choice but to remove every bit of waste from their operations.

You can learn from this industry. Search on the Internet for lean manufacturing or Six Sigma, and see what you find. Consider joining a group that focuses on lean. I joined the Association for Manufacturing Excellence for that reason. I bought books on lean and continuous improvement; I included tools on lean in the Mindshop toolbox, and I taught them so that I would become an expert in their application.

Great leaders are always curious; they are always looking for patterns and trends in consumers, businesses, and their teams to discover new ways to solve problems and capitalize on opportunities.

My next challenge is to become an expert in something else. I see it needs to be about communication, which includes use of communication technology, public speaking, and negotiation skills. Who do you think exemplifies best practice in communication? I admire writers like Napoleon Hill, speakers like President Kennedy and Martin Luther King, and for technology, the developers of Skype and the accounting software firm Xero.

I can study all these communicators, but it takes time. I estimate I spend at least ten hours per week researching and learning about communication in some form. I see it as an investment in my future. I love doing it, but I also need to be disciplined with it. I could easily spend all day researching gadgets like smartphones, but I also need to study speaking, negotiating, and psychology. I have, like you, limited time, so it has to be a balancing act.

If communication is my next best-practice need, what is yours? Whom and what do you need to study? How will you make time to invest in best practice? How long will you need to wait to get a return on your investment?

What You Can Do Today—Look at Other Industries for Best Practice

1. List the companies that exemplify best practice in your industry and what you can learn from them.
2. Determine what your next big opportunity for improvement should be. It is likely to be either a profit- or growth-related issue.
3. Research which companies in the world exemplify best practice in this area. Note five things you want to learn from them.
4. Do not attempt to push more business through an incapable system. Work on continuously improving your processes rather than simply working harder. Learn from the best in the world; there is little stopping you from being as good as, if not better than, them.

Chapter 24

● ● ●

Protect Your Personal Brand

What is your name? Mine is Chris Mason. Are you proud of your name? What does it stand for? What will it stand for in the future? Would you protect your name if someone attacked it? Your name is your brand. What is the name of your company? What does it stand for? Would you protect this name?

Back in 1986 when I started my business, I made a mistake. I had to select a name for my company, and I called it Chris Mason & Associates. At the time, I thought I was the biggest asset the company had and that the name needed to reflect that. I probably liked the thought of having something named after me, so ego also played a part.

In 1994, I realized that naming it after me was a mistake, so I created the name Mindshop. I knew by then that the company was more than just me; it was me; my wife, Julie; my son James; my customers; my team members; and my future. I saw it outlasting me. I always advise people to name their companies something other than themselves in case they ever want to sell the business; in my case, though, I knew that selling the business was unlikely to happen. I was building a dynasty.

Mindshop is a great name. I had the vision of "mind" shops of the future, where people would be spending money on products and services to develop their minds. Our name would last a long time, past my lifetime. But the name Mindshop means more than products; it also stands for integrity and innovation, and it's global.

Every time you interact with another person, it impacts your brand. If you are not clear what it stands for and how you will protect it, you will end up with a brand that stands for everything and at the same time stands for nothing. Customer service is an investment in your brand.

Some people will take advantage of your need to protect your brand. My advice is to think of the long term and, in the majority of cases, turn the other cheek to these people. We had a situation where someone had left Mindshop, kept claiming he was still a member, and was using outdated Mindshop resources on his website. We sent a letter of demand asking him to remove our material, which he did. In another case, a person was also using Mindshop material, but he was using it correctly and saying he had been trained by Mindshop, which he had. In this situation, we did not act.

We work very hard to get the right sort of people into Mindshop and to keep "users" out, but occasionally some poor-quality people slip in. Make sure you have mechanisms to identify these mistakes. This applies to both staff and clients. We rely on feedback from other Mindshop members; they are usually quick to let us know when members are not fitting. We then keep a close eye on them, looking for examples of an ill fit. For us, the language they use will often indicate that they are in Mindshop for what they can get out of it and are not willing to give anything or share with other members of the Mindshop community.

You can protect your brand with a clever design of your business model. In our case, with a senior experienced personal coach, high-quality members, unique methodologies, and no price increase since 1996, we make it difficult for others to copy us. With Coca-Cola and Pepsi, which have similar products and presence in the market, the ability for retailers to swap products is maximized. We don't want that to happen to Mindshop.

We do trademark our brand, but it's a question of how much trouble you would go to in order to take legal action against anyone infringing on the name and the brand. I see it as a deterrent, and most people infringing on it are small and insignificant to us, even in their local markets. I am more interested in improving our intellectual property so fast that competitors can't keep up, even if they had the research capability and unlimited funds.

Protecting your brand is all about continuously improving your service and quality performance. We attempt to double our value proposition each year (while holding the price constant). It requires us to question all our costs and activities. The bottom line is this question: "Does every dollar and every activity contribute to the value our clients need and get?" I think all of them do, so then it becomes a matter of which dollars and which activities generate the most value.

You must be prepared to make changes, such as removing services and activities that are of lower value to allow investment in new and higher-value activities. It doesn't mean an either/or situation. In our early years, we invested heavily in developing our toolbox and multimedia resources. Once we had that, it was not as costly to maintain it, freeing up the resources for employing our coaches. Our travel costs have always been high, but as technology improves, we are winding back our travel budget and increasing our marketing expenditure. The increased marketing activity protects and develops our brand.

What You Can Do Today—Protect Your Personal Brand

1. Select a name for your business that will live beyond your time in the company.
2. Register any trademarks.

3. Design your business model so that competitors will find it difficult to copy you.
4. Select activities that contribute to the value proposition, and once they are established, look for ways to redirect that investment to a higher-value activity.
5. Select the right team members and customers, and be prepared to remove anyone who doesn't fit with your brand and core values.

Chapter 25

● ● ●

Don't Worry about What You Can't Control

D o you control your business and personal environment? When things go wrong, whose fault is it? Your answer to these questions indicates whether you have an internal or an external locus of control. People with an external locus of control are people who blame everyone else for their situations. You will hear them saying things like, "If it wasn't for my staff, I would be profitable," or "I just can't find good team members," or "The competition from offshore means no one in our industry can make money anymore."

People with an internal locus of control will say things like, "When I invest in more training for my team, my sales will increase," or "I lost that person because we didn't look after him well enough." These people feel that they control their own destiny.

You can tell what sort of person you are dealing with by simply listening to what he or she says. Although you can help most people, those with a serious external-locus-of-control issue will be such hard work that it is probably not worth the effort. You are far better off letting them go and recruiting people with an internal locus of control.

Do you have an external or an internal locus of control? Listen to yourself. Why not record some of your conversations with others and listen to yourself? There is no need to record the other person; it's all about what you think and say.

I get asked a lot, "What if my spouse has an external locus of control?" Then the option of dismissing him or her is probably not desirable! There is a way of resolving it, but it will require a large investment of energy. What if someone says, "I'm hopeless with technology; I'll never master computers"? If he or she is a significant person in your life, then what you could do is to meet the person halfway. Start off by saying things like, "I'll do it. Have a look at what I've done," and then say, "Let me show you…" and then, "I'll help you do it; it's easy to learn."

This approach slowly nibbles away at the issue. Locus-of-control issues are usually too big for one quick fix. It will take you time to resolve an issue or even to modify it for yourself or those around you. You can be a positive influence on a person, but you will need to be patient. Your consistent and nonthreatening approach can help turn an external-locus person into an internal-locus person. It will take time, so practice patience.

What if the person concerned is a customer or supplier? In this case, your approach could be the same as that used with your spouse, but you need to question if you are prepared to put this level of effort into the person. If your customer or supplier has an external locus of control, it makes life very difficult because such people rarely take responsibility for anything that goes wrong. It is often easier to simply change customers or suppliers.

If you have a staff member with an external locus of control, your approach is probably somewhere between that of the spouse and the external-locus customer or supplier. You need to decide just how much effort you are prepared to invest, but keep in mind that 90 percent of people can be changed into internal-locus individuals. I suggest that with your staff, you invest more time than you would for a customer or supplier. This increases the probability of success and, at the same time, sends a good message to other members of the team.

The starting point is you. I think of myself as an internal-locus person, but I know that when I am tired, I can react as an external-locus person. This means that it is in my own interest to not get overtired. I need to design my schedule to minimize the long days, although it is not always possible when you work during the day and travel at night. Since I have cut my international travel down, this has become less of an issue.

If you hear yourself talking like an external-locus person, then take stock of your situation and identify what is causing this attitude. Are you overtired, is someone negatively impacting you, or is it a specific problem that is dragging you down? Whatever it is, deal with it! You may need help, and that's why at Mindshop we provide everyone with a coach.

For you to develop a company with an internal locus of control, you and most, if not all, of your staff need to have an internal locus. Assist each of the people who report to you to develop an internal locus. Show them how to develop the people who report to them into internal-locus people.

Recruiting people takes on a different perspective once you understand the importance of locus of control. Your interview questions can test for locus of control. It is much easier to hire internal-locus people rather being an expert change agent with people who have an external locus of control. Ask questions such as "Why didn't you get promoted further in your last company?" or "What stopped you from completing your degree?" And then listen to their answers. In an instant, you will know which type of locus of control they have.

If you have an internal locus, your family members have an internal locus, you've employed people with an internal locus, all your customers have an internal locus, and your suppliers have an internal locus, you will have a can-do (anything) life. Just being aware of the concept can be the start of resolving the issues in your life or capitalizing on new opportunities.

What You Can Do Today—Don't Worry about What You Can't Control

1. Make a list of all the key people in your life, both at home and at work.
2. Determine for each whether they are largely external- or internal-locus-of-control people.
3. Decide which of the external-locus people you want to assist to become internal-locus people.
4. Develop simple actions for each. Look at anyone potentially joining you at work as a staff member, customer, or supplier, and ask the questions that will test whether the person has an internal or an external locus. Reject anyone with an external-locus-of-control issue.

Chapter 26

●　　●　　●

The One-Page Plan

One of the tools we use at Mindshop is what we call a one-page plan. When I first started as a consultant in 1986, I believed in quantity and quality. I knew my reports needed to be informative and innovative, but I also believed that they needed to look like they cost what I was charging for them. Around thirty years ago, I remember picking up a plan, mentally weighing it, and deciding to add more appendixes to add bulk to it.

Today we don't place much importance on the plan; we sell the outcome, not the plan. If a client needs a profit improvement of 50 percent or a sales growth of 30 percent, then that is what we are selling, not the document that outlines how we are going to do it.

This change of thinking happened very early in my consulting career. I remember the precise event that caused it. My client and friend, Tim O'Brien, was managing director of a large manufacturing company, and I handed him his completed strategy for an aspect of his business. He took the plump plan, placed it on his desk, took his coffee cup and placed it on the plan, and said, "At least this plan will stop my coffee cup from marking my desk." I didn't say anything at the time, probably due to embarrassment, but that evening,

I realized that the plan was of little value to him. What Tim valued was my advice and support, not my ability to write a hundred-page plan.

Around that time, a Mindshop colleague, Warwick Cavell, came up with the concept of a business plan that would fit on one page. And although the layout has changed a bit, Warwick's concept has stuck and worked well for us ever since. Initially, we had resistance from the government and the banks, which were more focused on bulk, not outcomes, but over the twenty years or so since we launched our one-page-plan concept, there has been a realization that it is all about outcomes.

The plan is simple. Imagine a single page. The top left is where we are now, and the top right is where we want to be. The bottom half describes how we are going to get there. This "now, where, how" concept came from the Australian government and its World Competitive Manufacturing program; we effectively merged both concepts. There are other attempts on the market to produce a one-page plan, but they seem to fall into the trap of making the page big enough to accommodate many key performance indicators and other superfluous data.

We now use one-page plans for everything, starting with a one-page plan for the organization, one for each department, one for each function, one for each project, and even one for each person. We call this "cascading the plan." For the traditionalists, we also still append, where applicable, budgets and financial projections, documentation of tools used, research findings, and the like, in order to provide further context to the plans. The one-page plan as an outcome document is very easy to write and even easier to update, which is where the true power lies. We are finding that more and more accounting firms are adding a one-page plan as a summary to their clients' key financial statements in order to record their strategies and action plans.

We suggest updating each one-page plan every eight weeks. There is as much thinking required in a one-page plan as there is in a hundred-page plan;

the difference is the time saved in drafting and modifying the plan, which is significant. The eight-week cycle ensures a short-term focus and a corresponding short-term application of focused energy from all concerned.

It is the updating process that is the major benefit. The traditional business plan is bulky but normally prepared as part of some structured planning process, so there is plenty of initial energy available. The problem is that by the time comes for it to be updated, the enthusiasm has waned. With the one-page plan, updating is simply a matter of the removal of any completed actions and the addition of any new actions.

When used as a personal plan format, the one-page plan becomes a great focus for a career plan or performance review. As part of an employee attraction and retention plan, the one-page plan can be a key point of difference. I have my own personal one-page plan, and I also develop plans for each of my projects.

The one-page plan provides a focus on the key issues. It lists who is responsible for completing the action plans. It states clearly when things need to be done. It takes twenty minutes to write and five minutes to update. Storing the plans on the Mindshop platform enables me to share each plan with trusted others, which helps with the plan content and the accountability needed to make sure there is timely implementation of the action strategies contained in the plan.

What You Can Do Today—The One-Page Plan

1. Write a one-page plan for you.
2. Write a one-page plan for your organization and one-page plans for marketing, sales, operations, human resources, and finance departments.
3. Consider using one-page plans for all your key projects.
4. Consider one-page plans for each of your key customers.
5. Consider a one-page plan for every member of your team.

Chapter 27

● ● ●

Watch Out for the Energy Vampires

Have you read *The Celestine Prophecy*? Written by James Redfield in 1993, it is a great book because it explores how important energy is to us and suggests that we "steal" energy from one another using one or more techniques. There are the "Poor Me" people who are always complaining, hoping to get our sympathy (a form of energy). There are the "Interrogators," who aggressively question everything we do, aiming to put us on the back foot and thereby stealing our energy. Then there are the "Intimidators," who are the bullies of the world who steal energy by emotionally beating us up. The last group is the "Aloofs," who make us take the first move to invest energy into the relationship with them.

You need to learn how to avoid these energy "vampires." If, like me, you are a giver of energy, the energy vampires will suck you dry. You can tell when you are with a vampire even after just a few minutes because you will feel absolutely drained at the end of the meeting or conversation. Are there people like this in your life? If so, you need to develop strategies to protect yourself from them.

Make sure you have lots of spare energy: eat right, sleep well, and keep fit. Pace yourself during the day by building gaps in your schedule to walk, stretch, and eat. I always seem to have spare energy, even when putting in twenty-four-hour days when traveling. I do this by making sure I take little naps whenever I can, whether I'm flying, sitting in an airport lounge, or relaxing at home.

Yesterday I ran three workshops via the web. Even though the first one started at ten in the morning and the last one didn't start till ten in the evening, I protected my energy levels by lying down at nine in the evening for just fifteen minutes and taking a nap. When I woke, I felt great, and it showed in the responses from the participants in my last session. It was after midnight before I finally got to bed, and I bounced out of bed at six the next morning, ready to do it all again.

Your workload often has a cycle to it. My overseas trips tend to be around two or three weeks of long days, working most days and traveling most nights. I attempt to build spare days each week so that I can catch up on e-mails or just sleep. I make sure that the first week or two back I also take it easy to give my energy levels a chance to build back up.

Your physiology is directly linked to your energy levels. Think back to when you felt highly energized over something. It may have been a breakthrough at work, buying a new car, or just having lunch with a close friend. If you had videoed yourself at that time, what would you have looked like? Your body was probably standing tall, and you were standing more on the balls of your feet. Your eyes would have been opened wide, and you would have had a smile on your face. This process can be reversed. The high energy levels created the physiology, and if you can create the physiology, then the high energy appears.

The lesson here is to watch your deportment and your attitude. Act energized to be energized. If you find your energy levels dropping at a time when you can't nap, change your physiology and tap the energy that way. Recharging your energy batteries several times a day is essential. It's a bit like the battery on your laptop computer. You don't let it run down completely; you monitor it, and when it gets below about a third of its strength, you charge it up again. When your personal energy gets low, you also need to recharge. There are several ways to do this.

Doing work that you enjoy and meeting with people who are fun will boost your energy. It's not illegal to only do the work you enjoy and only mix with people who are fun to be with, but it is hard to manage. Start monitoring what energizes you and what drains you. When I do that, I end up with two lists that look something like this:

Energizes Me	Drains Me
Walking on the beach	Doing administrative-type work
Eating healthy food	Meetings that are boring
Naps when tired	Spending time with...
Laughing	International travel
Spending time with...	Gray skies
Driving with the top down	
A blue sky	
A good cup of coffee	
Working from home	

The next steps are easy. Work out ways to do more of the "energizes me" stuff and less of the "drains me" activities. It's not rocket science; it's all common sense. You have passed the test when you can say that you feel just as good on a Friday evening as you did first thing on Monday morning. Energy is a state of mind, but it is also about wise management of a valuable resource.

What You Can Do Today—Watch Out for the Energy Vampires

1. Make a list of the energy vampires in your life. Develop a plan to spend less time with them whenever possible.

2. Make a list of the energy givers in your life. Develop a plan for spending more time with them.

3. Develop a plan to eat well, get plenty of sleep, and exercise moderately. Pace yourself, and when your battery gets low, spend time charging it up before attempting the next project.

Chapter 28

● ● ●

If Your Education Is Finished, You Are Finished

As I covered briefly in chapter 3, I worked for the Electricity Trust of South Australia (ETSA) in the sixties. The personnel manager of ETSA was a former mathematics teacher named Hartley Searle. I remember him saying, "An employee who believes his education is finished is finished." What a great statement. I want to explain to you in more detail why it is such a good mantra to live your life by.

I've never forgotten those words and have done my best to live by them. I had eighteen years of tertiary education, a couple of them because I repeated subjects I didn't work hard enough at the first time around. I love learning, and I still feel a bit embarrassed about failing as many subjects as I did in my early years.

Your education does not have to be in a structured format; a lot of my most valuable learning came from my reading. I continue to read a lot, but my tastes in reading have changed significantly over the decades. In the seventies I read about technology and management; lately I've been reading about technology, business tools, and philosophy. I will always enjoy my reading, but now I get to read what I choose to read, which makes finding the time for reading even easier. A list of books that I have found valuable is shown in appendix 1.

I am so pleased that I enjoy researching technology and that this has been a constant in my education for so long. I estimate I spend at least two hours a day studying the latest trends in technology, particularly the knowledge I can use to improve my business and myself. Most people I know spent a lot of time on education in the early part of their lives and very little now that they are in senior positions. They may do an odd course or seminar and even read a book a year, but they are comfortable learning "on the job" and with their formal education to date.

Knowledge is available to us through so many avenues, such as our computers and smart devices. Not many families around the world today are without a computer or smart device under their roofs. With ever-evolving search engines like Google, you can find anything very quickly and learn about whatever subject you can dream of. You can search libraries with just one click. Videos make the learning easy. Your children and grandchildren take all this for granted; they can operate a computer at age two.

I guess what I'm saying is, there's no excuse for not investing time and money in your self-development. The emerging technologies make accessing other people easier, and exchanging ideas and knowledge is also educational. At Mindshop we have set up a chat area in our platform where our members can post questions and answers and share their intellectual property. I call this education just as much as studying for a degree at your local college or university.

Speaking and writing are also educational vehicles. You don't really understand anything until you attempt to teach it to someone else. Part of my job at ETSA was to teach apprentices electrical isolation procedures. When I was taught the subject, I accepted what I was given with few questions;

intellectually, it made sense to me. I remember in one class, however, I got one of those "But why?" questions that young minds are so good at asking. That challenge made me go right back to the basics and figure it out before I could answer the question. It was only then that I even started to know about isolation procedures.

Whom do you talk to, and what do you talk about? I am very fortunate to have a diverse group of friends globally. Julie and I spend up to seven months of each year traveling and learning. I believe you are what you know and whom you know. The people I mix with are never satisfied; they want to know more so they can do more. I surround myself with people who have knowledge and skills I don't have. I now listen more than I used to thirty years ago because the people around me are worth listening to. The more I listen, the more I learn.

As I get older, I recognize what I don't know, and I want to learn. What I need to know but am not interested in learning leads me to seek out others to advise me. If I combine what I know with what all my friends know, there isn't anything that comes up in my life that is an issue. Most of the people around me are smarter and more knowledgeable than I; what I have is lots of experience, a problem-solving mind-set, and a good general knowledge base.

I completed a PhD in industrial and organizational psychology, not because I want to be addressed as "Doctor," but because of the rigors of the formal learning and because I have at least fifteen to twenty more years of working ahead of me during which to apply the knowledge. My only barrier in doing a PhD was time, but I sorted that out. I had a fifty-hour-a-week job, and that wasn't going to change. A PhD takes around eight years of thirty-hour weeks of study and research. I decided I would have to invest eighty hours a week to maintain my job role and study at the same time. At the end of the eight years, I would have a PhD and know not just about psychology but how to research. The other option was to just stick to my day job. I am so pleased I decided to do both and must thank my wife and my boss (my son

James, who is Mindshop's managing director) for supporting that decision over the eight years.

The PhD resulted in new study and thinking habits, and in hindsight, that is one of the key benefits I got from my investment. There are lots of things I'd like to know more about—marketing and strategy and biographies of certain people come immediately to mind. Thank goodness my education isn't finished, or I'd be finished in Mindshop! How about you?

What You Can Do Today—If Your Education Is Finished, You Are Finished

1. Do an audit on the amount of learning you are currently investing in. All you need to do is estimate how many hours per week you invest in reading nonfiction material, researching, taking courses, or teaching others. Are you happy with the answer? Would you like to increase the investment?

2. Think about whom you mix with, what you read, and what you would like to know more about. For you, the answer could be emerging technologies, parenting, languages, or public speaking. Whatever it is, start researching how you can learn more, what courses you need to take, and what knowledge you need to acquire.

3. Invest just one hour each day in learning a topic of most importance to you, and see how it feels. Just reading this book for a few minutes each week will help.

Chapter 29

●　●　●

Guard Your Time Carefully

Do you realize that if you work for an organization, 80 percent of the value you are to that organization is generated in only 20 percent of the time you work? Even worse, do you realize that if you have a family, 80 percent of the value you are to your family is generated in 20 percent of the time you spend in family activities?

Yes, the Pareto principle is alive and well in your life, especially in where you spend your time. Everybody claims that the biggest issue in their lives is a lack of time, yet if Mr. Pareto is right, they could free up 80 percent of their time. Lack of time is never an issue; it's all about how well you guard your time.

Whenever someone tells me he can't deal with my issue because he is too busy, what I hear is, "What you want me to do is not a high priority." There is no problem with that; it is completely his call as to how he invests his time. But I wish he would stop using the excuse of having no time.

I have plenty of time. I use it to relax, to think, to be strategic, and to achieve things. I even do things for other people that I consider nonstrategic, but I decide what I do and when. I never tell people I am too busy; in fact, when I tell someone my schedule, and she responds with, "You are very busy," I say, "No, I have plenty of time."

I know you will become what you say and think. I have plenty of time because I do what I want and mostly only what I really want. There is no way I would say I am busy. I love having time to escape the noise of day-to-day "busy" activity. If I added up all the things I do that other people would consider work, then some weeks I work more than one hundred hours. Other weeks my hours of work would be as low as twenty hours, which means in any year I work somewhere between twenty and one hundred hours a week.

The key to time management is to guard your time. Consider time like money; don't waste it, and spend it wisely. You have a choice as to how you spend your time. If you had a choice to spend your time sharing an intimate conversation with someone you really care for or spending the same amount of time attending a boring meeting, which would you choose?

Learn to say no to people who want you to do low-value things with your time. This doesn't mean you have to say the word "no" in doing so. For example, when someone from the Mindshop network asks me for a meeting to resolve an issue, I suggest that she should first use the problem-solving tool called a force field to pull apart the issue and then send it to me. The normal response after completing the force field is, "I don't need to meet with you now. I've solved it."

Isn't that a nicer way of saying no to the meeting? The bottom line is, I guard my time well. Look for ways you can guard your time today. Imagine if you could free up half your time. If you could, how would you spend this time? Would you like more time to sleep, perhaps to read, to go to the gym, or even to spend time with your family? Did you know you can do this? It's not against the law.

Create the habit of questioning everything you do. Make more time for you. Stop doing the low-value activities. Apply the Pareto principle to your time. Make a list of the high-value activities, and make another list of the low-value activities. Estimate the amount of time you currently spend each week with the low-value activities. Don't be shocked if you find it is as much as twenty to thirty hours per week.

You can use this wasted time to do the high-value activities. Try it for just one day, and experience the benefit. If you like the feeling, then do it for one more day. Keep extending the goal until you create a new time habit. The key is to find innovative ways of saying no to low-value activities.

At the start of each year, I aim to create a vacuum of 50 percent in my work time. I delegate some functions to good people on my team, and I stop doing certain activities. Once I have half my time freed up, I have choices as to how I spend this time. What I have found in recent years is that what gets sucked into the vacuum are things like strategy, customer contact, reading, and time for me.

The bottom line is that each year, Mindshop and I become more and more successful. I have lots of energy, and people tell me that it shows. I know I have spare energy, and I am more than happy to share my spare energy with the important people in my life.

Once I am using my time wisely, I then look at the balance in my life. As noted in chapter 17, I consider that there are six key areas where I can invest time: family, finance, health, mental development, my philosophy/belief system, and social life. I make sure I don't spend too much time on any of these or ignore any.

You will be asking, "Where is work in his life?" I work with my family to create money, to stimulate me mentally in a way that fits with my belief system, to enable me to learn, and to mix with people I enjoy being with. In other words, work is the vehicle I use to create my six life-balance areas. All are equally important. How well are you guarding and investing your time?

What You Can Do Today—Guard Your Time Carefully

1. Start by applying the Pareto principle to your time. Make a list of the high-value activities you would like to do more of and another list of the low-value activities you would like to do less of.
2. Stop doing or delegate the low-value things for a day, and invest the time in some high-value activities.
3. Create a vacuum in your life, and watch it fill with strategic activities. Make sure you balance your life, investing equally in your family, finance, health, mental development, philosophy/belief system, and social life.
4. Create a new habit of guarding your time, first for a day, and then keep adding days until you have a new time habit.

Chapter 30

●　●　●

See the Best in People

Think about someone you love. If this person is a child, all the better. We seem to easily see the good points in a child; with adults, we filter what we see and comprehend. What do you like most about this person? Does he or she have any bad points? Do these bad points matter to you? These bad points normally don't stop you from loving the person. I consider this unconditional love.

It sounds weird, but you can experience unconditional love with everyone in your life. When I look at people, I see them as 80 percent strengths and 20 percent not strengths. I don't want to use the word "weaknesses" because that is not how I think. I see the strengths, but the weaknesses don't exist for me.

When you see only the best in people, it changes your life. You focus on the positives, and you start thinking more about teams. With a team, you can make sure that someone's 80 percent strengths are covering everything you need. It doesn't matter if I have any weaknesses because the focus is on my 80 percent strengths.

I know what my strengths are. I am strategic. I see things very early, well before most people. I energize people. I think and act quickly. I leverage these things well by making sure that most of my time is spent in these areas. I also know what I'm not strong in. Finance is of no interest to me. I'll listen if you tell me how much is in my bank account, but send me a balance sheet or profit and loss statement, and I normally won't look at it.

I want to be known for my strengths; I surround myself with people who are good at the things I'm not. That's why I'm surrounded by accountants! I like having them there. I know that 20 percent of my strengths generate 80 percent of the value I am to Mindshop. I aim to spend most of my time doing these things.

You can't see the best in other people if you can't see the best in yourself. You have to like and respect yourself. When I am facilitating groups, I use an exercise to get people to focus on their strengths. I call it the pairing technique.

Once everyone is paired up (with twenty people, we'd have ten pairs), I ask each person to think about the person I have paired them with and to make a list of ten to fifteen things they like about that person. After five minutes, they compare lists. They find it particularly refreshing to be told what is good about them.

I ask them how it feels and also whether that's how they normally feel at work. The difference is that I created a positive culture; we normally work in a negative culture. You can start to change your culture then and there. For a negative culture to exist, you need at least two people. You can't put down someone to just yourself. If someone starts a negative conversation with me about you, be assured that my response will be, "Have you told Jim? Telling me won't help, but I can suggest how you can tackle this issue with Jim."

Gossip is a cancer. Don't play the gossip game. Focus on the positives in a person. If someone denigrates a mutual friend, dispute the statement and respond with, "But don't you think...?" That sentence not only stops the gossip; it also replaces it with a positive comment.

You will find that focusing on only the strengths of others (and your strengths) gives you a culture of unconditional love. Once you have tasted this, you can never go back to a normal culture. The best part of all this is that you can start immediately.

What You Can Do Today—See the Best in People

1. Make a list of everyone important in your life. Write at least five strengths next to each name. Keep adding names, even people you have met for the first time today. Refuse to play the gossip game; it takes two to gossip, and if you won't play, the gossiping stops.
2. Make a list of at least five of your strengths. Focus on them, and start attracting people into your life who have strengths you are missing that are critical to your current and future roles. Consider the team, not the individuals. Make sure someone in the team covers everything you need.

Chapter 31

● ● ●

Control Your Ego

I am not sure I'm qualified to write about this point because I have yet to resolve ego fully for myself. I don't care that I am taking a long time to fix my ego issues; my ego is partly responsible for me being a good company director and for my having had the courage to establish a new business more than thirty years ago.

I am not saying erase your ego; I am saying control your ego. Overuse of the ego can be negative. You can tell if you are out of control with your ego by counting how many times you use the word "I" in a sentence. Try to say something without using the word "I." It is not easy.

The other way you can tell if your ego is under control is to watch the reaction of your audience whenever you speak. If you see them nodding with a "me too" expression on their faces, you are likely to have your ego under control. If you see your audience shaking their heads with a "so what" look on their faces, it is likely your ego is out of control.

As well as watching people's body language, you can also tell if the people you are with have an ego issue by listening to what they say. We have already said that what you need to do is minimize the use of the word "I." Listen to how often they say the word "I." If you notice they think everyone they know is an idiot, then it is likely that they think they are much better than everyone else, in part due to not having their egos under control.

The key is to see yourself as an equal—not worse and not better—equal but different. We are all at different places in our own journeys. Seeing yourself as an equal is an Australian trait. I guess it stems from our convict heritage. Most of the early Australians came from the United Kingdom, where there was (and still is) a class system. Once they arrived in Australia, there was no place for classes; there was too much pioneer work to do.

I traced my roots back to my ancestor George Mason, who stepped off a boat on December 9, 1842. A cobbler by trade, George established his business in Adelaide, South Australia (where, for the record, I was born in 1949). In those days, the population of South Australia was around thirty thousand people; in 2017, it is close to 1.3 million. In 1842, everything was controlled from London, and it took months to get a letter to London and months to get a reply. It was faster to sort things out, whatever the issue, independently of London. I think this DIY self-sufficiency has remained in the Australian DNA ever since.

We Australians still need that independence trait. We are on the other side of the world from much of the business action; to get to London or New York takes a full day. It's what we have to do if we want to build relationships in Europe or North America. Technology is making it easier to do the follow-up and service delivery, but relationships—the key to long-term business—need face-to-face contact.

Our lives go in cycles, and our egos are significantly impacted by these cycles. Age is a cycle: birth, childhood, puberty, adolescence, adulthood, marriage, children, grandchildren, old age, and death. Businesses tend to follow the same age cycle, except some experience a rebirth in the old-age stage through innovation, new ideas, new people, opportunities, and growth to build strength. Controlling the collective ego is a key success factor in business and personal growth.

As I have gotten older, I have accepted me for what I am—not perfect but unique, just as you are. Where my ego is strong, I leverage it; where it has a negative impact, I either control it or hide it. I have surrounded myself with family and friends who balance my ego. My wife, Julie, is an expert at pointing out my ego faults in a nice way. I might not always agree that I am at fault, but I recognize her views as being representative of the significant others in my life.

Mindshop itself also has an ego, one that is, thankfully, a composite of the many hundreds of people who are part of it. We can be confident, modest, caring, and fun to be with. We are not arrogant, defensive, cruel, or self-centered because of our collective ego. The collective ego controls the negative aspects of each person's individual ego. Step over the line, and the group will deal with it using direct communication, humor, and even a touch of sarcasm.

Some organizations are known for their egos. Microsoft and IBM have been seen as arrogant, but they didn't start out that way. What changed for them? Where are they today? Leadership is the major influencer of corporate ego. Think for a moment of the leader of your organization. How would you describe his or her ego? Now think about the public perception of your organization's ego. Is there a link between the two? Is there a need for change? Are you the leader? How will you change?

What You Can Do Today—Control Your Ego

1. Write down all the descriptors of your ego. Your list may contain descriptions such as confident, caring, ambitious, domineering, aloof, independent, fun, modest, and distrustful of others.
2. Now think of your work role. Which of these ego descriptors are dominant? Are you happy with where you are? What needs to change? Can you control the negative traits? Can you add people to your team with the missing elements?

Chapter 32

●　●　●

Develop a Leadership Mind-Set

Are you a leader? Before answering yes or no, think about your role at home, at work, and in your community, and then ask the question again. Are you the leader of your group? I'm not a leader in my community. I am a leader in my business but not "the" leader. I am a leader in my family. I am a leader in my industry.

It would be great if I could hear your answers to this question because they would tell me a lot about you. We respect leaders and have the belief that the leader gets more rewards than the followers do. I'm not sure that is correct. My thought process in the previous paragraph demonstrates that my leadership role is dependent on where I am and who is around me.

I always took the lead when I was young. On reflection, I felt that this approach gave me control, and I figured it was better for me to control what was going on. Then I joined the Australian Army Reserve around 1968 and was subject to the structure of "ranks," where a captain outranked a sergeant. The reason I joined was that the Vietnam War was in full force, and Australia was supporting the United States and its allies. The law at the time was that if you signed up for six years in the reserve, you didn't need to do the eighteen-month full-time military service.

I signed up, and when I revealed I had training as a surveyor, they immediately said that the artillery was the place for me: Thirteenth Field Regiment, Keswick Barracks, Adelaide, to be precise. So, Gunner Mason, military number 415557, was on parade and learning how to fire weapons of all types. I also learned how to exist on just a few hours' sleep per day, eating dehydrated food packs each day for weeks at a time.

The most important lesson I learned was that informal authority was stronger than formal authority. At one stage I was promoted to bombardier (corporal) and was responsible for a command post where we calculated the settings for the guns. I was good at my job and rarely made mistakes. Over the years, I saw a constant flow of officers who were technically in charge of me, but I actually called the shots on day-to-day operational issues.

In reality, I was the leader, but to an outsider, I was the follower. I liked having the control and the respect and the recognition I had even as a lowly bombardier; that was more than enough for me. I learned to respect our colonel (who was a judge in civilian life) because he was a great communicator. I respected our sergeant-major because of his strong discipline, and I respected one of my captains because he was prepared to admit he didn't know the answers.

We all were leaders in our own way. I could learn from each of the others. I realized, however, that if I was the leader of my pack, then I wasn't learning anything. I maximized my learning when I was surrounded by people who were better operators than me (in some key way). Whenever I felt I was getting to be the best at something, I knew it was time to add some more people to my circle of friends who could teach me something new about leadership.

I've applied this to my work life as well. I've found a lot of new faces in Europe and North America. Take the Americans, for instance. I wanted to know how they think and do business, so I started spending a few months a year visiting with them. I still do. I'll keep going as long as I keep learning.

Are you adding people to your contact list? They could be English, Scottish, Welsh, French, Dutch, a New Yorker, a Minnesotan, or a Singaporean. What people are you learning from?

I also like learning from the very young and the very old. I always say, "You are born perfect, and you die perfect; it's just that you are screwed up in the middle." I learned from my children even when they were young. I still do. After all, each of them is married, with two children, and they have lots they can teach me. They are members of Generation Next, our future leaders, and what they want is different from what baby boomers like Julie and I want.

To develop a leadership mind-set is simple. If leadership is what you mostly think about, then you will automatically adopt a leadership mind-set. Whether you are leading from the front, from within the organization, or even remotely, it is still leadership. If you are sharing expertise, coaching others, mentoring, and teaching, you are leading. Your leadership may be in a community, family, or business.

I get more excited about the reflected glory from helping others lead than leading from the front. Maybe I need to revert back to the experience of Bombardier Mason 415557 and just live on informal authority, learning how to fire new weapons such as virtual reality, augmented reality, machine learning, and artificial intelligence. What about you?

What You Can Do Today—Develop a Leadership Mind-Set

1. Read all you can on leadership.
2. Look for ways you can help others with their leadership opportunities.
3. Keep watching other leaders, and learn from them. Add more people to your circle of friends who can teach you something about leadership.
4. Leading by example will encourage others to follow you.

Chapter 33

● ● ●

Trust Your Intuition

Are you intuitive? Fortunately, I am, and I use my intuition most days. I went searching in 1995 for a course on intuition, and in Chicago, I found what I needed. (It wasn't a course, but it turned out to be even better.)

I went to a specialist psychological bookshop on the Golden Mile and told them I was looking for books on intuition. I was then directed to a local Borders bookstore (still around at the time!), and when I walked in, my jaw fell to the floor. The mega-bookstore concept had not yet hit Australia, and I couldn't believe there could be so many books under one roof. I went up to a sales assistant and told him what I wanted. He typed my request into his terminal and announced there were many books on intuition, and he then escorted me to where they were shelved.

He left me to spend the next hour collecting book after book: intuition manuals, everything I needed. I hit my credit card hard and had to buy an additional suitcase to get everything home. I ended up reading every book, finding out that what I wanted wasn't there, and then writing my own business intuition manual. It was a turning point in my life.

Many of the early Mindshop advisors will say that taking my business intuition course in the late nineties was a turning point in their lives, too. As more people joined Mindshop, we watered down the course due to some criticism of it at the time, but I could be easily convinced to offer it again. The controversy was mostly due to some of the tools I used to tap a person's intuitive ability—tools that included dowsing with pendulums, reading tarot cards, and tossing coins. I wonder what you would think of the course.

Let's see how you cope with a simple intuitive tool. Think of a question that has a yes/no answer but that you don't know the answer to. It may be something simple like "Should I buy a new car?" or even something more significant, such as "Should I stay in my marriage?" If you don't know the answer, get a coin out and say to yourself that heads means yes, and tails means no. Now toss the coin. When you see how the coin toss ends up, observe your instant reaction. It is this instant reaction to the coin that is your intuition at work. There is a 50:50 chance of getting heads or tails, so that is not the issue. Suppose the coin turned up a no to buying the new car—what was your instant reaction, relief or disappointment? That answer is the intuitive one; trust it.

All of us have the ability to be intuitive, but we have so much noise in our lives that we can't hear the intuitive inner voice. The noise comes from self-talk, worry, jealousy, and negative thinking in general. If you monitor your self-talk throughout the day, you will hear this noise. Removing this noise not only improves your intuition but also gives you a more positive outlook on life.

Meditation is a great tool for removing the noise. When you meditate, you can stand aside from yourself and not be part of your thinking. As the thoughts flow in, you can wrap them up and watch them float away. Once the thoughts stop, the noise stops. Sleep is also a good noise-reduction process. As I lie in bed, I remove the noise, and when my mind has calmed, I think of a specific issue, such as "growing the North American market," and add the thought, "When I wake, I will have lots of good ideas on how to grow this market." It is exciting to wake in the morning with flashes of inspiration. The key is to write them down before you lose them.

I mentioned that I have also used such different intuitive tools as dowsing and even tarot cards. Dowsing is a general name for a technique that uses a pendulum. Imagine holding the pendulum and telling yourself that if it swings in a north–south direction it means yes, and if it swings east–west it means no. You can then ask yourself a question you genuinely don't know the answer to, such as "Should I get a master's degree?" The pendulum should begin to swing, and if it swings north–south, the answer is yes. The rationale behind this is that your subconscious knows the answer, and your subconscious moves your hand to make the pendulum swing without you being aware of it.

The answers that come from a deck of tarot cards are not literal answers to your situation; rather, you need to focus on your response to the tarot answers. For example, the tarot card the two of pentacles is supposed to mean "It's a time when money and energy are likely to be available for new projects." If I drew this card while considering the issue of growth in the North American market, I might then think of stopping an investment in the Netherlands to free up resources to enter the US market. It's not what the card told me to do, but upon reading the card, it is the idea that came to mind. I then put that idea into action. Of course, I will never know if shutting down the Dutch market was a correct decision, but I do love working in the North American market!

You will find your own methodology for tapping your intuition. For example, it may be something as simple as soaking in a hot tub and reflecting on your issue. If this practice works, then use it whenever you can. Learn to trust your intuition and practice it often, and you will become an intuition expert. The more you practice it, the better you will get at intuition.

What You Can Do Today—Trust Your Intuition

1. Remove the noise in your life by using meditation or any other tool that works for you.
2. Maintain a journal of your intuitive insights, even if just for a month, so you can check if your intuition is working.
3. Practice using your intuition as much as possible. Practice makes perfect.
4. Google the word "intuition" and read anything that intuitively interests you.

Chapter 34

● ● ●

Your Purpose in Life

Do you know what your purpose for existence is? I do. The advantage of knowing your purpose is that you'll know what to say yes to and, even better, what to say no to. The following is the purpose statement I wrote in January 1994. It still works for me today. Keep in mind that at that time, I hadn't started taking any of my world trips, and Mindshop had just started. In some ways, it has become a self-fulfilling prophecy.

I am…

* the best publisher of business and personal processes in the world.
* a world citizen traveling and living wherever I can provide the maximum value to others.
* a provider of support and inspiration to those closest to me, my family and my friends.
* continuously developing my skills, knowledge, and understanding through trust in myself.
* prospering and sharing my wealth and happiness with others and so rewarding myself.

I can show you a mechanism for determining your purpose. In fact, I can give you two ways to do it. If you are a logical-thinking type, then the first method should suit you. Write a paragraph on each of the following: your work, your money, your relationships, your knowledge, and your family. Just writing a paragraph is harder to write than a page because there is no room for padding. Stick to the facts.

Now go back five years. Where were you then? Write a paragraph on each of the five key areas of your life as they applied five years ago. What has changed over the past five years? Now go back another five years and repeat the process. Keep going back at five-year intervals until you were born. It's not an easy task. It will take time and may require several sittings.

Once you have written everything, read it all again, this time trying to "connect the dots." In other words, look for the connections, the patterns between the key events in your life. What you should see is that your whole life is "on purpose"; what you thought was bad is, in hindsight, good because it pushed or pulled you somewhere and you ended up where you are today. Whether good or bad, every incident is a learning experience. Once you see it that way, the negative experiences seem more easily absorbed.

Look at where everything is heading. If you can identify the trend lines, you will find they all lead to your purpose in life. When I do this exercise, I find such key events as working in my father's small business on school holidays, learning self-discipline (and how to exist on four hours of sleep a day) in the army, my first export trip to China in the mid-1980s, and of course, meeting my wife, Julie. Adding in the births of my three children, my education, jobs in training, and a technology background, and it makes complete sense why Mindshop does what it does and is heading where it is heading.

I find it comforting that there is a reason behind everything, that there are no accidents. The people you meet are all there for a reason. I have learned that some people come into your life and stay, and others come into your life and go. All are important. A chance meeting with someone for just five minutes may deflect you to a major opportunity.

The second method probably will appeal to the creative/visual people. This time, draw a line sloping up to the left. The slope of the line represents your growth because the vertical axis is performance and the horizontal axis represents time in years. In the middle, draw a vertical line representing today. Think back over your life and draw in any key event that has impacted your journey. As before, you will see the links and realize that your life is already on purpose. Extrapolate the line (hopefully it is sloping upward), but this time, develop key events that will have a positive impact on your future. In the past, it was probably a combination of good and bad experiences that impacted you. In the future, we want to maximize the good experiences and minimize the bad ones.

You may find that this line points to your purpose in life. This exercise did that for me. I discussed mine earlier in this chapter. Once you have a purpose statement worked out, reflect on it for a while. We put mine in a frame and hung it in the office so I or anyone else could look at it and ponder its meaning. It's better if it is not too specific. But it needs to cover all aspects of your life—it's your life purpose, not just a work purpose. I think mine is great, and I have no plans to change it.

A key benefit of a purpose statement is that it reinforces what to focus on, what to say yes to. An even better benefit is that you also know what to say no to. I have found that the key to being on purpose is to say no to much of what you are asked to do. You can tell when you are on purpose; you are in the flow, and you get lucky and keep finding opportunities to improve your life and the lives of those around you.

What You Can Do Today—Your Purpose in Life

1. Use one of the two purpose tools just described, and develop your purpose.
2. Post your purpose in a prominent place to reinforce what you need to focus on.

Chapter 35

● ● ●

Embrace Life's Barriers

What are the best bits of your life so far? You are probably thinking of events like a marriage, the birth of a child, graduation, promotion, buying a house, or even learning a skill. What are the worst bits of your life so far? Now you may be thinking of things such as a death in the family, being sacked, a breaking of trust, losing money, sickness, or maybe failing at something.

I have grown significantly and continuously over my life, and events such as failing eleventh grade of high school, breaking the state record in the four hundred meters in 1965, joining the Australian Army Reserve, marrying Julie, and the birth of our children were times when my growth peaked. It also peaked when I worked for the Chamber of Manufacturers and again when I left the agency to head up Laser Lab Limited. I think starting Mindshop UK in 1996 would rate a mention, as would James and Emily each joining the family business. Our fraud experience, while unpleasant, did cause many positive changes, as did my giving up consulting to become a coach of consultants.

Each of these events, the positive and the negative, provided me with positive outcomes and growth opportunities. Each was a barrier that I had to face and overcome. Barriers are how you grow. I could even say with hindsight that the negative events produced more change and more positive outcomes in the long term.

The lesson out of this is to manage the barriers rather than just let them happen. When I was the CEO at Laser Lab, I faced a situation that at the time I considered to be a major barrier. I had to go to Shanghai to address a conference of two hundred laser engineers on how to make money from lasers. The trouble was that, back then, I didn't even know how lasers worked. I was highly stressed, and it showed. I felt overloaded with work and had no time for anyone. A few days before my flight, a friend called to say he had a major issue with a trade union and asked if I could help. Within seconds I had planned the fix for the problem and offered to come to the factory and take charge of matters. My friend then said, "Aren't you flying to Shanghai this week?" My response was, "I am, but I can still get this done." He then admitted he had made up the union problem to show me how insignificant my travel issue was and that I was stressing over nothing. I certainly learned from that lesson.

I like the saying "Things that don't kill you force you to grow." I now create my own barriers. One personal barrier is that I want to have a business that generates $50 million in sales with a 20 percent net profit. I don't care if I live to see this outcome because I believe we will get there. Our strategies and actions reinforce this goal. We think and act like a $50 million business, which means we will ultimately get there. This size of business was a big barrier for me because I didn't want my family to be negatively impacted by the wealth that comes with it. I am now convinced we won't change, even if we do grow to $50 million, so it is no longer a barrier.

A business of that size will create other barriers, such as how we control it, what technology we will need, how will we staff it, and what products and services will be required. These barriers are also easily resolved through lots of hard work, but that's not intellectually difficult. The key is to break each barrier down into small, achievable steps and to keep implementing no matter what happens so that over time, the big-step improvement happens. Each barrier is a learning and growth opportunity. The steadily increasing capability coming from facing barriers ensures that my ability to face future barriers without fear of failure is enhanced.

What You Can Do Today—Embrace Life's Barriers

1. Plot out your life, and list each of the key events that have impacted your life.
2. Envision where you want to be in the long term, and work out what barriers you could set for yourself that will force you to grow both personally and in a business sense.
3. Once you have identified your barriers, break them down into small, easily achievable steps, and then keep going. Barriers are growth opportunities; welcome them into your life.

Chapter 36

● ● ●

What Is Your Success Equation?

In a previous chapter, we talked about happiness; this chapter is about success. How do you define success? It all depends on where you are in life's journey. If you have just been in a serious car accident and have temporarily lost the use of your legs, success for you is probably being able to walk again, something others take for granted. The only definition of success is the one you set for yourself.

For me, success is about life balance, because for most of my working life, I probably have not had good life balance. It would be interesting to know what your definition is. I have always defined success as having the money and time to go anywhere (and do anything) you want in the world at any time you like. Having the time to do this is more difficult to achieve than having the money.

I designed my company and my job to give me the time and money to travel, so I have been successful according to my original definition of success. As I have matured, I have become more spiritual, and I now believe that life is all about what you are becoming. Personal growth is what drives us; it's just that some people don't want to drive themselves any harder than they need to.

I love to read, and I love to write. Until now I have mostly read and written for myself, but today I also read and write for others. I consider myself successful, and I will continue that success by sharing my knowledge and experience with others. Not everyone will define success as I do, and that is good. Many will define success in financial terms. How important is money to you? You can test this by making a list of all the people you know who are successful.

Who is on your list? Why are they on your list? When I think of the people on my list, they are people with life balance; they have great marriages and good kids, and they give back to their communities. And, yes, they have enough money. How much money is enough? Enough for me is having sufficient funds to live the life I want with some left over for a rainy day. You can only sleep in one house at a time.

I do prepare a balance sheet of my financial situation every now and again. My balance sheet lists my assets and my liabilities, and my logical aim is for the assets to be considerably more than the liabilities. My key goal is for my net position to be continuously growing. I work a similar process for the nonfinancial aspects of my life. I list under assets what I know, the people I know, the relationships I have, and the value I have provided to others. On the liabilities side, I list the mistakes I have made and my weaknesses. And, I am happy to say, I believe I have a very healthy personal balance sheet. I do want the net nonfinancial assets to keep growing each year, just as my financial assets do.

When you look at your balance sheet(s) and compare it (them) to others around you, are you the leader of your pack? I think there's a problem when you are the most successful person in your circle of friends or even in the top 25 percent. The reason why it's a problem is that if you are the most successful person you know, whom will you learn from?

Keep in mind that I have defined success as life balance, so those I look up to are those with good scores for each aspect of their lives: family, finance, health, mental development, philosophy/belief system, and social life. So am I surrounded by a lot of people doing better than me in all these areas? Probably not. I have added a twist. I know a couple of people who are doing well in each area and lots of people who are doing well in a few of these areas. I admire the balanced people and learn from the others in their areas of expertise. You can learn from many of the people in your life if you take the time to get to know them. Make a list of the six life-balance areas, and list people you know in each area who do better than you.

You may find that you can list people in several of the areas and not in others. That may mean you are the leader of the pack in those areas. Your challenge is to add to your circle of friends in the areas where you are strong and to learn from your friends where you are weak. Let's assume you have friends who are stronger financially than you are. Work out ways to get them to help you. Ask them how they do it. Read what they read about finance and business.

Where you are already strong, let's say in the area of mental development, you will need to attract new people into your circle of friends who outperform you in that area. Maybe they are better educated, wider read, or just more intelligent. Ask for their help; find out what courses they took and what books they read, and see if you can meet their friends.

Before long you will find yourself continuing on the path to success, always surrounded by people who are better operators than you are. You can still help others as you go forward. This will tap the value-to-others mechanism that will prepare you well for your next success step.

There is no end to this—not in this life, in any case. Keeping your good friends, continuously adding new friends, and striving for a balanced life and more success is a great plan. Don't forget to help others with their success plans as you go.

What You Can Do Today—What Is Your Success Equation?

1. Make a list of the six life-balance areas—family, finance, health, mental development, philosophy/belief system, and social life—and list people you know in each area who do better than you.
2. Add people to your circle of friends in areas where you need to improve further.
3. Ask for their help, do what they do, and read what they read, and you will continue on your path to success.

Chapter 37

● ● ●

Profit Is King

"Profit" can be a dirty word for many people, but it never has been for me. I see profit as a measure of efficiency, because if your price points and service levels are good and you make more profit than your competitors, you must be efficient. For most established businesses, unless the profit is at an optimum level, why would you want to increase sales? If you are a start-up, it's normal to not make a profit initially.

Profit gives you working capital, peace of mind, cash in the bank, and a return on your investment. The profit enables you to invest in new products and services, an essential activity for long-term survival. Many people pay themselves peanuts, struggle to pay their bills, and never make a profit. Those people are almost better off staying home and doing nothing rather than working long hours for little or no return.

What frustrates me is that with just a little bit of strategy, discipline, tough decisions, and coaching, these people can dramatically improve their profit performance. So why doesn't it happen? Their dissatisfaction is high, but the vision for how their lives could be—and the plan for making it happen—is just not there.

More than fifteen years ago, I was invited into a textile mill in Australia to help the company sort out its profitability issues. I said at the first meeting, "I'll take it on, providing we are profitable within three months!"

The general manager's response was, "We haven't been able to do it in the past; why will we be able to now?" The mill had lived on cash injections from the owner and government subsidies for as long as anyone could remember.

We fixed it within the three months, in part because I believed we could. Up until then, those in the company hadn't believed they could, and they were right as well! Profit is a philosophy of the organization and a measure of an organization's self-worth. If, deep down, the employees think the organization is rubbish, then it usually follows that the profit is rubbish.

Of course, just believing we could do it was not enough. What we did was to start with a blank whiteboard, add the customers and the CEO, and redesign the structure of how to deliver our product to the customer. We found we had a hundred people more than we needed to do the job. Over the previous thirty years, the structure had been bloated by continuously adding a person or two every few months. The fix was as simple as pulling the spare resource out!

If you are in agreement that profit is king, then the next step is to get your profit trend lines moving in the right direction. Make a list of all the potential profit-improvement ideas. Beside each item, add three columns. The first is the likely profit improvement the idea will generate in the next year. The second column is how much profit will be generated in the next five years. This is not always simply five times the value in the first column, because some ideas provide all their improvement quickly, and others take a long time. The third column is for the words "easy" or "hard," which represent how easy or hard it will be to achieve the specified result.

The profit opportunities need to compete for your attention, and my advice for the first year is to take the items with the highest first-year value that are easy to do. This gives you a quick return for your effort, and as you develop your experience at continuous profit improvement, you can be more confident to take on the hard high-value items.

This process is a never-ending journey. Isn't that an exciting thought? In the short term, you need quick results; once you have built up a value bank, you can take more risks and even make a few mistakes. It is normally the old "two steps forward and one step back" outcome. Don't worry about the one step back; it's all about the net two steps forward.

You need to create a habit of continuous profit improvement. Question the cost of everything, and question any activities that don't contribute to the profit. Apply the Pareto principle by asking the following questions:

* Which 20 percent of our products give us 80 percent of the profit?
* Which 20 percent of our processes give us 80 percent of the profit?
* Which 20 percent of our customers give us 80 percent of our profit?
* Which 20 percent of our staff give us 80 percent of our profit?

Asking these four questions and studying the answers will give you lots of good ideas as to how to improve your profit. Profit is king. It is the reason we establish a business in the first place, and the profit must be significantly higher than the low-risk places (like banks) where you could alternatively invest your money. If you are an employee, then the same process works, except you will measure your "profit" for your investment in your time and expertise by counting your salary, benefits, learning, experience, recognition, and fun that come directly from your employment.

If you are an employer, there is a lesson for you in the last paragraph. Are you creating an environment where your people can "profit" from working for you and where you can "profit" from your investment in the business as well? The organization is a profit-generating black box. Your job is to keep tweaking the profit every day, every week, every month, and every year.

What You Can Do Today—Profit Is King

1. Start by making a list of your ideas for improving your profit, and compare them using the methodology I have described in this chapter. Always have at least one profit-improvement project on the go at any time.
2. Next, apply the Pareto principle to your profit, and that will help you generate even more ideas for your profit-improvement teams.

Chapter 38

●　●　●

What Are Your Three Key Issues?

I don't know about you, but I always have a long list of things I want to do, both at work and at home. How many issues do you have on your list? I have hundreds, and I am sure you do as well.

My favorite activity when I am assisting people in developing their strategy is to ask the following question: "If you had a magic wand and you didn't need to worry about how or the cost, what would you change about your...?" You can insert "business" or "marriage" or "life" or whatever into this question. My clients normally come up with a long list. I then ask, "How does it make you feel having so many issues?" and their answer is often "depressed" or "overwhelmed."

I then explain that there are probably three or four key issues on the list that are strategic; the others are likely to be symptoms of the fact that they have yet to fix their strategic issues! Why chase the smoke-and-mirrors stuff? Just fix your top three issues, and as you fix one, choose another from your list to take its place. Ideally, you should always be focusing on just the three most strategic issues in your life.

Mindshop's need for a simple diagnostic to work out which three issues became apparent to us many years ago, so we went about developing one. We called it our GPS diagnostic, with GPS standing for "growth and profit solutions." I remember exactly where I was when this name came to me. I was in a car with Mindshop's Gill Burn; her husband, Lance; and my wife, Julie, heading to Nottingham, England, to have lunch. As the car went around one of the thousands of roundabouts, we decided GPS (global positioning system) was a good analogy for our business because we needed something that told us where we were, where we wanted to be, and how to get there—just like GPS does in a car.

I offered to come up with the twenty-five questions and their weightings that would give a business its color-coded key issues out of a possible ten factors. Mindshop's managing director—my son James—experimented with the weightings, and before long we had solved it. The ability to be able to see what scores you needed and work out what areas you needed to work on to fix the business proved to be a valuable outcome. You don't need a diagnostic to decide what three issues are the most important ones. It is more important to make the selection and get on with fixing them. I am never sure whether the key issue I am working on is really the most important, but that doesn't stop me from working on it.

The part of this philosophy I like best is that it is a never-ending journey. You'll still be working on the next three strategic issues when you die. Imagine that you could resolve your current three strategic issues over the next couple of months and then repeat the process for a full year. What would your life be like after a year of resolving three key issues every two months?

What an exciting vision! The benefits are obvious. So why don't you do it? The answer for most people is that they are too busy working on fixing the smoke-and-mirrors issues, the symptoms of the fact that they are not fixing their three strategic issues.

Over the years, I have worked out why most people can't develop the discipline of being strategic. In a business, the reward systems are normally designed around the short-term performance activities; consequently, looking good at meetings, putting in long hours, networking with the right people, and minimizing problems with customers are thought to be more valuable than putting time into waste reduction, developing a staff-retention program, or coaching your people. These strategic issues are not as easily rewarded, so the leaders stick to rewarding the more visible short-term issues.

It is a challenge to link the rewards system with the strategic issues. Normally, it is easier to reward someone working in an area like sales, but how do you reward someone in administration or leadership? That makes it even more important to do so. When I think about the four jobs I have resigned from in my life, the common element in my dissatisfaction was that none of my bosses were interested in my views on the strategic issues for the business, let alone my own rewards and recognition needs.

The part I like best about the approach of focusing on the three key issues is that if I know I'm doing a good job on my three issues but am falling behind on any of the others, I don't need to feel too bad. Only my three strategic issues really matter. What are your three issues, and what are you doing to fix them within the next two months?

What You Can Do Today—What Are Your Three Key Issues?

1. Select the top three issues for your business and for yourself.
2. Link a rewards program to the achievement of them.
3. As soon as you complete an issue, select the next most strategic one, and you will never run out of issues.

Chapter 39

●　●　●

Build Your Memory Muscle

I use my memory every day. Memory is like a muscle: use it or lose it. I use my memory muscle to remember my travel schedule, the Mindshop tools, client facts, and people's names. Mindshop has a tool called the "seven learning principles," and one of the principles is called "overlearning." The definition of overlearning is this: "forgetting is significantly reduced by frequent attempts to recall previously learned material." I can recall this definition anytime I want because I do it at least monthly with a client.

If you remember back to your early days at school, this is how you learned the alphabet and your multiplication tables. If I ask you what six times six is, you will respond instantly with the answer: thirty-six. If I ask you what fifteen squared is, you may be able to just as quickly respond with the answer, 225, or you may have to spend more time to work it out. It depends whether you applied the principle of overlearning to knowing your squares like I did.

The advantage of being able to remember your multiplication tables is obvious because we use numbers in all aspects of our lives. Most people think I am mad to commit to memory my travel schedule for the next three months, but I do it for a couple of reasons. When I have quiet time and am planning my next trip, I find it useful to not have to fire up my computer or find an itinerary of my trip to be able to think through where I am going, whom I will be seeing, and what I want to achieve.

When it comes to remembering the Mindshop tools and processes, most people agree that it is a good thing to do. My clients wouldn't be impressed if I had to consult my computer or our online platform to answer their questions or provide advice on how to resolve their business issues. They like the fact that I carry all this information in my head. The point is, if you had been trained in the tools and processes, you would be carrying this capability with you as well. My advantage is that I can recall it all at will. What are some facts that would be a competitive advantage if you could recall them at will?

I believe everything we have ever experienced in our lives is stored within us—every sight, every noise, and even every feeling. I also believe that these experiences affect our beliefs and behaviors whether we can recall them or not. Having the ability to recall them is a distinct advantage in my job, as it is in yours. I remember the hundreds of Mindshop tools and processes in part because I believe I can and in part because I continuously attempt to recall them.

I do the same with people's names. People love it when you remember their names, and I love that I can; it's a win-win for everyone. When I meet someone, I repeat his or her name and link it to some other fact. If I meet someone called David and he reminds me of another David I know, I think to myself, "His name is David, and he looks very much like David Jones." I might repeat that five or six times upon first meeting David.

I was at a meeting of the Institute of Management Consultants, and I met someone I hadn't seen for a long time. I remembered he had been a client and what company he worked for. I had met his wife once, walking along the banks of the Yarra River in Melbourne, but I could not remember her name. When I first saw him, I could not remember his name, but my immediate thought was, "I can't remember his name, but if I relax, it will come to me."

By the time I had a brief conversation with someone else at the meeting and started to walk back to my seat, his name came to me, so I walked straight up to him and asked, "Are you...?" and he replied that he was, and he introduced my wife and me to his wife. Problem solved. The key was in telling myself to relax and that his name would come to me.

I force myself to remember names, and I suggest you do the same. If you trust your memory like I trust mine, think about what you can use it for. I use mine for the following list. Rate yourself on how well you use your memory for each item.

* people's names
* key facts and figures
* meetings I have attended
* details on people's families
* how to find my way when driving
* my schedule for meetings in the coming year
* phone numbers and codes

When I rate myself on this list, I do very well on them all except the last one, the phone numbers, and I know why. I have entered into my mobile phone all the phone numbers I may want to use, so I don't need to remember them. I don't even know my home phone numbers, and I believe it's because I know I don't have to know them. I agree it would be useful to commit them to memory; it is the lack of attempts to recall the phone numbers that is my problem. It is the many attempts to recall people's names, their family details, client facts, the Mindshop tools, and my travel schedule that has resulted in my excellent memory in these areas.

All you need to do is decide what would be good for you to be able to recall at will and then remove any safety nets. Force yourself to remember, and keep attempting to recall the facts and figures. The more you use your memory muscle, the stronger it becomes. Just start with a couple of important facts, and go from there.

What You Can Do Today—Build Your Memory Muscle

1. Make a list of some key things you would like to trust to memory.
2. Use "overlearning" to embed them into your memory.
3. Stop telling yourself what you can't remember, and instead tell yourself what you can remember.

Chapter 40

● ● ●

Making the Right Decisions More Frequently

Do you make good decisions? I do! Not because I am smart—I do because I have a decision-making process. Let's say I have had a great year in my business, and I want to upgrade my car. My process will ensure that I buy the best car for me. You can use the process to work out which is the best car for you. I use the same process for every important decision in my life.

Once you know that you need to make a decision, the first step is to work out the factors that are important to your decision. For me in this example, the factors would be performance, reliability, quality, price, style, and retained value. These factors are not of equal value. I find it best to restrict the number of factors to around ten.

The second step is to weight each of the factors to recognize how important you think each is. I normally make the total score one hundred points and spread these points over the selected factors. In my decision matrix, I would weight performance as forty points and price as five points. If you disagree with my weighting, then score your factors the way that works for you.

The third step is to score the first alternative, and I do that by allocating midpoints for each factor and, by so doing, make it the benchmark. So, my first option, a BMW M3, scores twenty points for performance and two and a half points for price.

The fourth step is to take the first factor and score all the cars using the twenty points I gave to the BMW M3 as the benchmark, and then repeat the process for all factors and cars.

The fifth and last step is to total the points for each car and see if the outcome feels right. Here is my first attempt at a decision matrix for buying a car. You can see I have followed all the steps, but the outcome of the Ferrari doesn't feel right. I think I know where I went wrong. I should have weighted the retained value and price higher and the performance lower. All the cars I have considered perform well, so I don't need forty points for this factor.

Factors	Weight	BMW	Porsche	Ferrari
Performance	40	20	25	30
Reliability	15	7.5	7.5	5
Quality	15	7.5	7.5	10
Style	15	7.5	10	13
Retained value	10	5	3	5
Price	5	2.5	1	0
Total	100	50	54	63

By adjusting the weighting and rescoring the factors, a much different result is achieved. This time, the decision is a tie between the Porsche and the Ferrari, which is probably right.

Factors	Weight	BMW	Porsche	Ferrari
Performance	20	10	15	18
Reliability	15	7.5	7.5	5
Quality	15	7.5	7.5	10
Style	15	7.5	10	12
Retained value	15	7.5	10	12
Price	20	10	8	1
Total	100	50	58	58

This happens more often than you think. Even if the difference is a couple of points, I consider it a tie. What I do then is two things. First, I literally sleep on it. I leave it for a day or so, and then I trust in my intuition. I can tap my intuition by using a simple intuition tool. Let's assume I've slept on it, I don't want to adjust the decision matrix scores further, and I really can't separate the two cars.

As I described in chapter 33 on intuition, my next step is to toss a coin. Before you laugh, tossing a coin can bring your intuition into play. I decide which option is heads and which is tails. It makes no difference, so in this case, I would say the Porsche is heads, and the Ferrari is tails. I then toss a coin.

It came up tails, the Ferrari. As you know, it had a 50 percent chance of coming up tails, so no surprise there. The important fact was that the instant I saw it was tails, I felt disappointed. Deep down, I must have wanted a Porsche. That is my intuition at work, so the answer is to buy the Porsche.

Keep in mind that I was doing this for real, so I now feel good about this outcome. If I think about it logically, I just confuse myself. I like the look and sound of the Ferraris, but I like the reliability and practicality of the Porsche. Thinking is noise. The decision matrix showed it was very close, and so my intuition had to be the decider.

I've used this decision-making process regularly over the past decade for a range of situations, including the following:

* buying a house
* buying a car
* employing someone
* deciding on business strategies
* selecting a client

Look for every opportunity to use this process. Make it a habit, because the more you practice it, the better you will get at it. It looks so simple that it's easy to discount it. A decision matrix ensures a robust decision process and reduces the negative impact of emotional thinking. I think it is in the top three Mindshop tools, and I don't care if it is simple!

What You Can Do Today—Making the Right Decisions More Frequently

1. Select an issue that you need to make a decision on.
2. Use a decision matrix to score the options.
3. Check by using a coin toss to tap your intuitive decision making.

Chapter 41

● ● ●

Tenacity versus IQ

I'm not that bright, but I am tenacious. I know lots of bright people who seem to not do that well in life. I think most tenacious people I know do well in life. If I had a choice of being bright or tenacious, I would go for tenacity!

I don't know who originally said, "The harder you work, the luckier you get," but it is true. I am lucky: everything always works out well for me, in part because I work hard. It's not just the hard work that makes you successful; it's about applying your hard work in the right place by being strategic. I guess that's why the fable about the tortoise and the hare has always appealed to me.

The analogy I like is drilling for oil. I see people wanting to get rich quick, so they start "drilling for oil" but get bored quickly and move their "oil rig" to another spot. In life, I see this happening when someone joins a company, makes a few mistakes, gives up, and moves to another company. What people like this can never know, and I can never prove, is that if they had stayed drilling in their original spot just a bit longer, they would have struck it rich. The real-life situation, in this case, could be finding you have a boss who is difficult to work with (the hard rock) and moving on, when all along the members of senior management were aware that your boss was not performing and were considering replacing him with you.

It is hard to test these theories because you can't test both alternatives concurrently, but my advice is that once you have committed to somewhere, someplace, or someone, hang in there. The grass always looks greener because you can't see all the problems in the other alternative. A lot of people keep moving all their lives, changing jobs and changing life partners in the hope they will find what they are looking for. They think deeply about their situations and can convince themselves that moving on is best.

Thinking is noise. Intelligent people think about all the consequences of each of their options. They think about what can go wrong. They can easily convince themselves of one option and then another. Not committing totally to one option leaves them susceptible to not effectively implementing any of the options. Tenacious people don't give up. Edison was tenacious, and so we got the electric light bulb. He saw every failure as knowledge: knowledge of what didn't work, which narrowed down his options. Most of the great achievers in the world just kept going at whatever they were doing until it worked. The problem is, you never hear about the failures, so it is easy to believe that Edison and others had something special that we don't. They were subject to the same probability of success that we are. What was the difference between Edison and an average person?

The difference wasn't some special talent or a gift of nature; it was through his tenacity that he succeeded. Where does this tenacity come from? Are we born with it? I think so. You only have to look at a baby's will to live, to escape his or her mother's womb, to understand tenacity. As children develop, you start to see them giving up, but I think that is learned behavior. Parents see their children becoming frustrated with a task and often take over and do it for them or use distraction to move them on to something less frustrating.

We can teach tenacity to our families and the people we work with through example. Instead of changing our business strategies every year to some new fad, we can dig in and develop a commitment to less exciting strategies such as customer service, quality, waste reduction, and effective communication.

Some managers see their role as "entertainers," always searching for new and innovative programs, but they are inadvertently teaching their people to not stick to the basics, that "fluff" is more highly regarded than "substance," and "more of the same" is automatically wrong. How many times do you hear, "We tried that before, and it didn't work?" In the training arena, we call it "edutainment," where trainers can rate well on the sessions they deliver, but the training has very little impact on the commercial needs of the business.

Imagine if you could combine tenacity and IQ—let's call it strategic tenacity. We stimulate and motivate our people with well-thought-out long-term strategies and the certainty that once we start something, we see it through to the finish. With such a culture, who would be attracted to work for us? Tenacious people would be attracted, and they are the perfect people to stay and be committed to a long-term strategy. Gone are the days that people stay with a company for life, but keeping your best people for as long as possible nonetheless remains a key success factor in any organization.

So if I'm right, does everyone need to be strategic? I would argue that if we had tenacious leaders (who were strategic) and surrounded them with tenacious, skilled people, we would have a great team. If that argument is correct, then we should be recruiting people with tenacious traits, and our reward procedures should be rewarding tenacity rather than IQ. Is this how your business is currently staffed and managed?

What You Can Do Today—Tenacity versus IQ

1. On a scale of zero to ten, rate how tenacious you are.

2. Share your self-assessment with someone you trust. Are there any significant variations?
3. Select something very important to you, and document what the outcome would be if you never gave up on it.
4. Develop and implement a plan for that outcome. Reflect on the personal benefit of being tenacious with all such important issues in your life.

Chapter 42

• • •

Don't Say "Try"

I was once told that there is no such thing as try; you either do or you don't. This thought has haunted me ever since. I now listen to what I say to myself and others, and if I catch myself wanting to say the word "try," I edit it out of my conversation.

For example, imagine someone asks me to do some research for him on leadership and have it to him by the end of the week. I catch myself about to respond with "I'll try to get it done this week." I pause, and then I quickly decide whether I am willing to get it done in time or if I need more time. Once I decide, I respond with either "Sure, the end of the week works for me," or "How about Wednesday of the following week? I can get it done by then." I replaced the word "try" with a positive response that gives the other person confidence in my future actions.

When my habit of saying "I'll try" was first pointed out to me, it was done in such a way that it had a lifelong impact on me. I was talking to a friend, and without warning, he asked, "Can you stop using the word 'try' in anything you say to me from now on?" I sat there for a long three or four minutes, and the only words that came to me were, "I'll give it a try," so of course, I had nothing to say! That awkward silence has haunted me ever since, and I am confident I have now removed the use of the word "try" from my vocabulary.

Monitor your conversations for the next day or so, and see if you have the same habit. Listen to what you say at meetings, while talking on the telephone, and in your general conversations with family and friends. You'll soon determine if you have the habit or not. You may also pick up on your use of other words and phrases that are not useful to you.

I think many people use the word "try" either when they are not sure they want to do whatever the other person has asked them to do or when they definitely don't want to do it but don't want to say so. The response gives you stress because you feel bad when you don't get it done for the other person, and it gives the other person stress because right away he or she is unsure of your intentions. No one wins in the "try" world.

The result is that others need to keep checking with you on progress, adding more pressure to both of you and wasting a lot of time. By removing the word "try" from any communication with others (and your own thinking), you gain energy because you have less worry and less stress. You may have to become comfortable with saying no to some requests as an alternative to saying, "I'll try." It's a valid response to many situations, but normally people feel uncomfortable saying no, so they use "try" instead.

You can head off the "try" situations with some anticipation. Let's say you have a meeting scheduled with representatives of a client company, and you know they are dissatisfied with how some work you are doing for them is going. Think about all the requests they are likely to make of you, and decide in advance whether you can help them or not and what a reasonable time frame to do the task is. You may even want to write them all down; consider it a risk-management plan.

If they raise an issue that you have already considered, you have an instant response and a time frame to go with it. If they raise an issue you did not consider, you may want to respond with, "I understand the situation, and I'll come back to you with an answer by the morning." They will respect you for making a considered decision, you have time to reflect on your options, and you have not had to use the word "try" at any time.

You will be surprised just how many times we say "try" at home. Your partner asks you to give your mother a call to invite her for dinner, and you respond with, "I have back-to-back meetings all day, but I'll try to call her during a break." A better response would have been, "No problem. Consider it done." Which response would you prefer when you ask someone to do something for you? "Try" is a bad habit we get into, and it's a huge time waster.

If you think the word "try" is an issue in your communication, you can fix it starting today by deciding that you will not say the word again. Censor everything you say and think. Just as you developed a habit of saying "try," you can develop a habit to not say "try." I'm asking you to do it—not to try to do it, but to actually do it. Are you up for it?

What You Can Do Today—Don't Say "Try"

1. Monitor your use of the word "try."
2. Each time you notice you are about to use the word "try," edit your words and replace "try" with "Sure, I'll do that," or even "I don't think that will work for me." It is all about creating a new habit.

Chapter 43

●　●　●

What Will You Stop Doing?

t is a fact that you have only 168 hours available to you each and every week. In my thirties, I managed some weeks to wrangle up to one hundred of those hours for work, but I found that was about my limit. Back then I equated success with hard work and hard work with the hours I worked. My rationale was, the more hours I spent working, the more successful I would be.

As I have previously commented, eventually I learned that the success came from a minority of the hours of work; in fact, when I learned the Pareto principle, it made sense to me that 20 percent of my activities generated 80 percent of my results. That made me think about what were the 20 percent of activities that I was doing that led to my success. Back then it was things like my ability to dictate reports and letters, my multitasking, and my reading. I then decided to do more of these types of things and less of the 80 percent activities that included driving and flying to appointments (and the office), administration tasks, and lots of my meetings. I decided what to focus on and what to stop doing.

This did not happen on a specific day; it was more of a transition over a year or two. Having a list of the things to (eventually) stop doing was cathartic. Once they were on the list, I just needed to wait until the opportunity to get rid of them or significantly reduce them became apparent. As I freed up more and more time, I was able to do two things: first, to fit more of the 20 percent items into my schedule, and second, to invest time in activities such as exercise. These small wins encouraged me to keep the process going.

I kept adding to the list of things to remove, some of which confused people around me. I decided that meetings and travel could be a waste of time, so I went home to work and made it difficult for people to meet with me face-to-face. I remember one client (and friend) e-mailing me to set up a meeting to discuss a problem he was having in his business. He was aware I was working hard at minimizing travel, so he offered to come to me and have the meeting at my home. The point he missed was that he was wasting time in driving and meeting with me. How I resolved this was to ask him to apply a couple of Mindshop tools to his problem and then send the results to me, and we could set up a call to resolve it. A few days later, I got an e-mail from him saying, "Don't need to see you; it's fixed!"

I did recognize in this situation that part of the reason he wanted to meet was social; he just wanted a chat. I waited a couple of weeks, and then I suggested that he and I and our wives should catch up over dinner, and so we met at a restaurant close to him. This was a great outcome. It didn't require me to invest work time because I used my social time, and my wife was part of the solution—a win-win for everyone concerned. In part, this dinner was a celebration for the client and me that we'd resolved his problem in a very time-effective way. He also learned that the solution to the vast majority of his issues and opportunities was in the Mindshop toolbox, not in meeting with me as he first thought.

This pattern of removing my 80 percent items and making time for the 20 percent got finalized about fifteen years ago. I began to review my job description every November and set an objective of creating a 50 percent vacuum in my workload effective from the first of January each year. That is where my personal effectiveness really took off! I actually announced that this was my new personal policy, so I was locked into doing it. Once I promised it, I was committed. I created this 50 percent vacuum in my work life with two main activities: delegate and stop doing. I probably should have mentioned the delegation part earlier; I had used a bit of this from day one. I found the "stop doing" activity harder to use, but delegation was effortless, providing I had good people to delegate to. I was in a position by then that all I needed to do was to suggest to my son James, our managing director, that I would like to get an activity off my job description, and it usually happened quickly.

There were other techniques I used as well. I aimed to touch things only once (we have all heard of that one). What I added was to touch it once, but leave it to the last moment to do it. You are probably thinking I am advocating procrastination; I consider it incubation. I mull things over both consciously and subconsciously. The difference between procrastinators and incubators is that when procrastinators deliver their work (late), it is of poor quality. Incubators deliver it right on time, and it is both insightful and of good quality.

I also do hard things every day, but I will do easy or fun things first to help me build momentum. Once I have the momentum and am in the flow, I make the next job something hard, something I have been incubating for a while. I find a nap for ten minutes midafternoon (if possible) often triggers a creative spurt for the rest of the day. I take walk breaks, even if only for a few minutes every hour. I have my Apple Watch set up to remind me to move every hour. Keeping the blood circulating seems to help.

I have a well-balanced life, and the policy of redefining my job description in November gives me something to look forward to each and every year. I plan to work at least another fifteen years (I am currently sixty-seven), but that will happen only if my work is exciting and rewarding. I love working from home, using technology to reduce travel time, and giving away some of my stuff to others so they can also learn. It's a great continuous succession process. Could this work, even in part, for you?

What You Can Do Today—What Will You Stop Doing?

1. Keep a log for just one week of your key activities.
2. Assess each for the value that activity provides you.
3. Make a list of the low-value activities, and work out ways to stop doing them.
4. Repeat the activity logging every few months.

Chapter 44

●　●　●

Your Exit Strategy

Do you know when you will be leaving your current job? That doesn't mean retire; it means when are you likely to leave the job you are doing now? In today's volatile and unpredictable job market, you can never tell when your job will end. The impact of technology disruption, global competition, business sales, mergers, or even incapacity through illness means we need to assume we may need to leave our jobs at any time. This risk can create a threat for you, your family, and your employer.

When studying for my PhD, I had the opportunity to take on some elective subjects, one of which was consulting. I figured that because I had been doing consulting for around thirty years at the time, it would be interesting to see how it would be taught from an academic perspective. I was expecting some surprises, but one of the first concepts covered was the need to develop an exit plan as soon as you start an engagement. The rationale was that if you did not assume you would exit, you would build a dependency relationship with the client.

I don't fully believe in that concept because it assumes a lot of impractical things: it assumes that the client will be able to find help for new and emerging issues other than you, it undervalues the need for a trusted relationship (which can take years to build), and it also undervalues the investment made in understanding the client organization, the market that it operates in, and the people who work in the business. What hearing that concept did do is remind me that the relationship would end one day, so a plan for that exit needed to be made whether you were a consultant to that organization or its leader.

I suggest it is a bit like playing chess: if you can see the next five moves ahead, you are more likely to win than a player who sees only the next move. If you know you will be leaving in exactly one year from now, how will that impact your plan for the coming year? I am suggesting that it is good to assume that the need to leave may occur at short notice, even if the probability is low. Issues such as succession plans, scenario planning, and planning for change become more important.

If you are a baby boomer, it is more logical to have an exit plan filed away somewhere, even if it is only in your head. I suggest that a well-documented plan shared with your other key people is a better idea. If you are a millennial, I suggest that you should also be planning your next move. This does not have to mean leaving the organization where you currently work; it can mean changing your current job role. Of course, the exit may be decided by your boss rather than you; in that case, you need to build in some job insurance.

You can build your job insurance plan easily. Think of someone you know who could get an equivalent or better job tomorrow if she got fired today. Would you be able to do that? Most people would not be able to. If you can think of someone with good job insurance, what are the things that provide that person with that insurance? It is likely to be things like being well connected, having good networking skills, having a good reputation in the market, being a team player, being a great communicator, and even being a good problem solver. Rate yourself on these and other factors; where are the gaps in your job insurance plan?

I've mentioned in several chapters that I plan to work for another fifteen years. What, then, is my exit plan? About twenty years ago I set up my plan, which states that my legacy to Mindshop is to be my contribution to the intellectual property, methodologies, and culture. To the Mason extended family, the legacy will be financial security through the provision of values, education, support, and encouragement to all family members. The "what" is easy; it is the "how" that has been more challenging.

With regard to the Mindshop legacy, the company's intellectual property (IP) has been documented in papers and videos (rather than being stored in my head as it was thirty years ago). I continue to participate, but now the Mindshop IP is generated by hundreds of people, not just me. The legacy must be a sustainable process, not an outcome. What is the legacy you plan to leave when you exit? Is it documented? Do others use it daily? Is it valued? This is a great opportunity for you.

To protect my exit plan, I continuously use scenario planning. My version of scenario planning is simple to use. I have a plan (which is integrated with my exit plan), and I test the robustness of the plan against several likely scenarios. These scenarios include radical technologies, no technology, loss of our key leaders, unstable economy, and a strong competitor entering the market. It is critical to have a plan that can withstand any of these threats and opportunities. My exit, planned or unplanned, will likely be inconvenient but not a threat.

To test my exit plan, I appointed a variety of leaders to run key parts of the Mindshop group, but it wasn't until my son James replaced me as managing director that I knew the plan was robust enough for long-term survival. I then slowly removed myself totally or partially from the key roles to see what happened. I figured that if it didn't work, then I could always jump back in. The key elements of the exit plan that I tested included such aspects as financial management, public speaking, coaching, growth, and of course, the long-term vision. When tested, all these elements confirmed that I was backed up, even made superfluous, by other people within Mindshop, primarily James.

What You Can Do Today—Your Exit Strategy

1. Assume you will exit your job in the next year or so. Make a list of what you need to do to ensure that the business (or your family) is not adversely affected.
2. Determine what your legacy will be when you go. Do you have job insurance? Could you go to another job within days if you lost your current job?
3. Integrate your exit plan into the overall business plan for your organization.
4. Test your plan for robustness against all the likely future scenarios.

Chapter 45

●　●　●

Focus on the Bright Spots

Are you a glass-half-full or a glass-half-empty person? Either way, if you play to your strengths, you will do well. The key is to do a better job of leveraging the assets around you. I call it focusing on the bright spots. It's OK not to be perfect. In my lifetime I have traveled extensively and interacted with people even at the prime minister level, and I haven't gotten to know anyone who is perfect. Some have done really well in life by playing to their strengths.

What are your strengths? If you had to name three, what would they be? What potential strengths have you yet to leverage? I consider my three current strengths to be my work ethic, my intuition or gut feel, and my self-confidence.

On the other side of the ledger, what are your areas of nonstrength? Mine are my ego, my financial analysis skills, and my fitness level (which fluctuates from time to time). I plan to turn these three nonstrengths into tangible strengths. I will explain how shortly. What are your nonstrengths?

How do you turn nonstrengths into strengths? My nonstrength of ego used to be a strength in the early part of my career. I consider that I progressed as a leader faster than most, reaching the level of CEO of an international publicly listed company by age thirty-five. I received a lot of criticism because people felt that I was too young to hold a job at that level. My ego became my protector, a force field that minimized the impact of the negativity of others. As I became older, the concern became less about my age and more about my being too egotistical. My protection became a source of renewed negativity from others.

Among your strengths could be your ability to communicate with others, a profitable segment in your business, your ability to motivate your team, or even your ability to set a vision for your organization. One of my strengths is having a vision for the future, both personally and in the business context. I remember being asked by a teacher when I was around eight years old what I wanted to be when I grew up. I can still remember my instant reply: "I will be an expert." I didn't know what I would be an expert in; I just wanted to be the best!

Whatever strengths you have, use them to leverage your opportunities and to overcome any threats you may have. Take my strength of intuition— how would you suggest I use that to leverage the opportunity I have in sharing my knowledge and skills with others? One way I am thinking of is to take my research skills and use them to deconstruct intuition, to learn how it can be developed and to teach others to be intuitive. I did that about fifteen years ago but without any research capability, and my efforts to teach it were limited by the fact that my intuition process was "intuitive" and not evidence based. It made it easy to learn for naturally intuitive people but difficult for those who need logic to be able to learn effectively. Well, I plan to do it again but with a more scientific approach, so watch this space!

If there are nonstrengths you have very little interest in improving, an op-tion is to delegate tasks involving these nonstrengths to others. In this way, the fact that you have access to this resource is still a strength. I am surrounded by people who have great financial analysis skills, so it is now a strength in my life, even though the strength is not within me. Building a team of people with complementary and required skills for the future is as important as building your skills. Life and business are too complex for any one person to contain every skill needed. This fact has encouraged me to look for people who need to add my skills of work ethic, intuition, and self-confidence to their team. Once on the team, I look for ways to transfer my skills to others—hence the need for me to teach and keep teaching. I owe my teaching skills to my five years in the Australian Army Reserve. It was there, in my early twenties, that I learned the principles of teaching others, supplemented subsequently by more formal training as I got older.

Another key thing to do when focusing on the bright spots is to hang out with people brighter than yourself. I don't avoid people based on their intelligence; in fact, I think I avoid people based on their values, if anything. I do consciously seek out bright people to hang out with. I love the challenge they bring to me; it means that I am constantly stimulated by the company I keep. Some of their brilliance rubs off on me. These bright people can be found in every coffee shop, where you work, among your customers, and even in people next to you on a flight. The key is to listen to them, look for their "brightness," and then engage them by asking insightful questions about them and whatever they are talking about. Look for the patterns and trends from the bright spots rather than the not-bright spots.

It is also important to catch people being bright. What I mean by that is to stop competing with people. When they say something bright, don't respond by trying to say something even brighter. Compliment them for the comment. I often respond to a person who has just said something clever with, "Wow! That is so good. Where did you learn that?" However, don't be an interrogator; people do not want to play twenty questions. You will learn more by listening than talking. Ask insightful questions, and the other party will realize that you are also bright and have something to contribute.

The bright spots can also be contained in any failures you have. Failure is a learning opportunity. When I plot the key events in my life, it is the so-called failures that, in hindsight, provided the most positive impact on me.

Don't feel bad about failing; look for the bright spot contained in that failure. After a while, you'll see the bright spots in every failure, in most of the people you meet, and in you. The challenge is to better leverage those bright spots.

What You Can Do Today—Focus on the Bright Spots

Here are six things you can do to make sure you focus on the bright spots in your life:

1. Make a list of your strengths and nonstrengths.
2. Work out how you can convert the nonstrengths into strengths.
3. Use these strengths to leverage the opportunities in your life and overcome the threats.
4. Hang out with people brighter than yourself. (It's easier than you think.)
5. Comment on any bright statements made by others. Don't compete with them; accept and recognize their brightness.
6. Look for bright spots in any failure you encounter.

Chapter 46

●　　●　　●

Fix the Root Cause (Not the Symptom)

I wish I had learned about symptoms and root causes earlier in my life. I spent most of my time back then fixing symptoms and not fixing what was generating those symptoms. I remember working for a client company that was experiencing a slow decline in sales; my automatic response was to show the client how to build a sales process, to train the company's key people in how to sell, and to coach the company's leaders in all these aspects. I missed the warning signs. What I now know as "external locus of control," where people tend to blame everything around them for their predicament, was such a warning sign. If my clients told me the problem was the customer, my response was to show them how to find "better" customers. If they told me the problem was "insufficient" funding from the bank, I went with them and got more funds approved. The actual problem, however, once I dug into it, was ineffective leadership. I was chasing symptoms and not the root cause.

I was fortunate to learn soon after about the tool called the 5 Whys (5 Ys). This technique is straightforward to use but difficult to master. You take the issue you want to resolve and keep asking why until you get to the root cause of the problem. The first of the 5 Ys in my previous example would have been, "Why are sales declining?" I then would have developed a number of possible reasons, but if I settled on lack of sales process as the likely cause, I would have asked the second why: "Why is there a lack of sales process?" By drilling down like this around five times, I would have found the response, "We have ineffective leadership." The answer often can be found after just three whys, but sometimes it can be seven. On average, it takes 5 Ys to find the answer. You know when you have found the answer because it is something you can fix, and the problem stays fixed.

In this case study, the root cause was ineffective leadership in the sales function, and that problem was performance-managed out. Given this leader, even if I had implemented a great sales process and provided sales training and coaching, it would not have worked. We had to change the leader first and then apply a sales process, training, and coaching. I suggest you apply the 5 Ys every time you are problem solving.

I mentioned earlier that 5 Ys is a hard tool to master. As with many of the Mindshop tools, you won't understand the subtleties of using the tool until you apply it around forty times. This tipping point is difficult to reach, often due to the need for instant gratification. Masterpieces take time to produce, and the art of becoming competent with 5 Ys also takes time. I assume you have plenty of problems to practice the 5 Ys on. The sooner you start, the sooner you will accumulate your forty attempts required to become proficient in 5 Ys.

One of the issues that makes 5 Ys difficult to master is what we call circular reasoning. If you are working on a personal issue with 5 Ys, you may find a potential answer to more than one of the Ys is "not enough time." This can cause a loop back to an earlier answer, but it can also be an excuse why you do not want to fix the real issue.

Finding the root cause is also essential to solving any of your personal problems. I encourage you to use the 5 Ys on personal problems as well as business problems. I was coaching a senior person working in an accounting firm. Her problem was how to get promoted to a partner role, which she felt was too difficult. She was a Mindshop person and so knew about the 5 Ys, but telling her to go away and apply the 5 Ys to her problem would have been unlikely to work. What I did was to weave 5 Ys into our conversations over a month or so, and in this way, I camouflaged my use of the tool. I then integrated another practice into my application of 5 Ys. If I asked her to make a list of two hundred prospects and she did not do it, I halved my request to one hundred contacts. If that had not worked, I would have kept halving my request until she did it. Once done, I then slowly doubled my request to reach back up to the original request.

In this example, it was the integration of the 5 Ys with the halving of the quantum of my original request that triggered an action. Success builds further success and increases confidence. You probably want to know what the root cause was in this woman's situation. I don't know for sure, but I think it was ineffective leadership again. Her superiors felt that simply defining the pathway to partner was sufficient; they thought if she was strong enough, she would make it. What they should have done was to watch closely her attempt at their process, coaching her through her successes and failures. They didn't do that; it fell back to me to do it. Maybe she would have made it anyway after a bit more time. It makes one wonder how many high-potential people have been lost to an ineffective leadership environment.

Another agent that masks the root cause is performance. The accounting firm in this example was performing well in spite of its ineffective leadership. If I had challenged the leaders that their leadership practices were significantly limiting the performance of their firm in terms of profitability, client service, and even employee engagement, they would have laughed at me. The skill is in driving the required change in spite of this ignorance. Even though I understand the factors that contribute to ineffective leadership, I am experienced enough with the 5 Ys to have an informed opinion of what the root cause is. I find it more effective to keep this knowledge to myself and be more patient with how I apply that knowledge.

The sales problem and the promotion issue may sound familiar to you. Even if you have a sales problem or a promotion issue in your life, it will be very different from these two examples. The difference comes from the different people, the different environment, and even you being different. It is the 5 Ys tool that will effectively handle these differences.

What You Can Do Today—Fix the Root Cause (Not the Symptom)

1. What are the three key issues in your life today?
2. Apply the 5 Ys process to each.
3. Are there any common root causes?
4. Develop plans for the root causes.

Chapter 47

●　●　●

Carry the Wounded, but Leave the Stragglers

I consider loyalty to be essential for an effective organizational culture, but it is not provided at any price. I assume that everyone deserves my loyalty until it is proven that they don't deserve it. People who deserve my loyalty will have these characteristics: they are a good values fit, they have a good work ethic, they are team players, they continuously improve on their value to me and the organization, and they learn from their mistakes. If they also have the characteristics of being fun to work with, well liked by customers and other team members, and reliable, that is a bonus.

If I sense a person is in breach of any of the key characteristics, I try to ascertain whether his or her problem is a temporary issue, such as a health or an emotional event. Even then, if I am not sure, I will test the situation. Some time ago I was working as a consultant to a large international manufacturing organization. My role was to assist the company in developing a strategic plan and helping to implement that plan. The number two leader of the organization was the production manager, an affable man who had been there for twenty-six years. I sensed that he was blocking the change process, but I was not sure why.

The test was simple: confront him with my suspicion, and watch his reaction. Some of the older readers will remember the television series *Columbo*, about a Los Angeles detective with the appearance of a bumbling and disheveled policeman, but in reality, he was a dogged investigator. When he cornered his targets, they lowered their guards and thought they were going to get away with their crimes. But Lieutenant Columbo doubled back and trapped them into confessing their guilt.

My version of the "Columbo technique" is to confront people and accuse them of the crime, and when they plead their innocence, to apologize, walk away, and watch what happens after that. With my production manager suspect, I found an excuse to chat with him (I think it was about football), said goodbye, and started to walk away. Then, unexpectedly, I turned back and said, "By the way, I've been thinking about your role in our change process, and I get the impression you are blocking it."

His immediate response was, "You've got to be joking. I'm your biggest supporter."

My response was, "Sorry, my mistake."

I then waited and watched what happened. If I was wrong, he would have just shrugged it off, maybe even becoming a bit more visible in his support of the strategy implementation. Unfortunately, he didn't do that. He actively tried to get me removed from the organization, talking negatively about the change process and me.

My next step in the Columbo technique was to repeat the conversation but this time with the CEO. His response was, "That's not right; he's been here for twenty-six years and is a good friend of mine."

Again my response was to walk away, saying, "Sorry, my mistake."

Now it was getting interesting. What would the CEO do? He started watching the production manager through the filter of "he is blocking the change process." What he observed was that the blocking was indeed happening, and he fired the production manager in due course. My loyalty to the production manager was terminated as soon as I had confirmed the negative impact he was having on the organization. The only risk for me was to get removed from the project, but if the production manager had been able to do that, I was never going to be successful in any case.

If the production manager had come back to me, saying, "I've been thinking about what you said, and I can be more supportive of the change process," my loyalty would have gone up, and the CEO would never have been alerted to the problem. I would have classified him as "wounded" and done whatever I could do to carry him. He proved he was a "straggler," however—that is, someone who is not even trying to help (hence the title of this chapter, "Carry the Wounded, but Leave the Stragglers").

With any wounded, I do whatever I can to support them. The stragglers I let fail, knowing that I directly told them the problem they were causing and the impact it was having on the organization. I encourage you to do the same with your stragglers and to make sure you are never a straggler. When you are working on a project, why not go to your boss and/or an external consultant and make it clear you are supportive of the change and would like to help more?

I need to make it clear that firing stragglers is only a last resort. Other exit strategies include moving the person sideways, demoting the person, or simply removing him or her from the specific project. Change is difficult at any time, and the stragglers are taking up valuable space and consuming valuable resources, and thus they put the change project at risk. Building your team is a trial-and-error process; weeding your organization by removing stragglers and supporting the wounded is a key success factor in business.

What You Can Do Today—Carry the Wounded, but Leave the Stragglers

1. Make a list of the wounded. Work out how to support them.
2. Make a list of the stragglers. Work out how to remove them.

Chapter 48

● ● ●

Family Must Come First

I think I could be considered an authority on family: I founded a family business that has been operating successfully for thirty-plus years, I have been married (to the same woman) for around forty-five years, I have three children and six grandchildren, and somehow it all works. It works because we all share the job of making it work. Our common employment is just the vehicle we use to work and play together. The difference is that in the family there is unconditional love; you don't normally get that in a business. This unconditional love makes our business strong, and it is why we adopt value to others as our key belief.

If you have read chapter 17 on life balance, you know that family is one of the six areas of your life that you must keep in balance. I have lost count of the number of successful businesspeople who failed to maintain that balance; some effectively recovered and got it right on their second (or even third, for some) try. You can tell what your emphasis is by auditing where you spend your time. How much quality time do you spend with the family? I don't count sitting with family and watching television—I mean, how much time do you spend interacting with family members?

The Mason family is fortunate in that we all live in the same city, so access is relatively easy. Even so, the members of each family unit are busy with their own commitments, and it is not easy finding quality interaction time. Working in the same business is helpful because we are each in communication daily while working on a common purpose. Geographical location and a common purpose certainly help, but so does our use of technology. Phones, e-mail, Facebook for some, and FaceTime or Skype are a daily occurrence. We have regular family dinners (whole-group dinners are normally for special events) and celebrate Christmas, birthdays, and births together. We also catch up regularly with each family unit. In between all that, we do some work, but family comes first.

I demonstrate my belief that family comes first in many ways, but one aspect is particularly telling. If any of my grandchildren ask me for time, the answer is an automatic yes. It may be to watch them play a computer game, to play basketball or darts, or even a request for a sleepover at our house. The benefits of this policy are obvious. As in business, the Pareto principle (20 percent of activity generates 80 percent of the benefit) applies. Our grandchildren want quality time with us, and this is because we are fun to be with, we have the right equipment (dart board, basketball hoop, Xbox One, iPads, smartphones), and we treat them as being very important to us.

I think it is all about commitment. I am committed to my family, more committed than to anything else in my life. I demonstrate the commitment daily by continuing to work in the family business when many of my peers have already retired or have been retired by their employers. This outcome does not happen easily; threats to the family need to be identified early and managed quickly.

One of the threats to a family is the introduction of new members to it. As our children married, Julie and I made sure their partners were welcomed. We engage with their families, and we aim to be role models for them and their children. If they need our support, we automatically offer it. We don't impose that support; we offer it. The offer is just as important as the support itself. We anticipate needs, we fight over who pays for dinner, we get criticized for being too generous with our gifts, and above all, we show we are interested in their lives.

I have clients who are estranged from one or more of their children. They fight over money, their marriages have split, there are contested wills, and deep down, they don't like one another. This will be the outcome unless you manage the threats early. I learned early in my family life that when a threat arises, someone needs to take responsibility for fixing it. Sometimes that person needs to be me, but we all share the role. The hardest threats to resolve are those that involve emotion. In those situations, someone needs to offer an olive branch or even turn the other cheek. What is more important, winning an argument or maintaining family harmony?

I choose family harmony every time. I believe that I need all my energy to help others. Therefore, it is best to not have family issues dragging at my energy. And I can assure you, that never happens. If on occasion I have missed an early warning sign from a family member, I deal with it as soon as I become aware of it.

Think about your relationship with your best friend. What are the essential ingredients for your special relationship with that person? Your list may include things like trust, love, fun, mutual interests, mutual friends, and mutual support. That is a pretty good list for family members as well.

Family issues also arise that you have no or little control over. These issues include things like the death of a family member, long-term health problems, or even failure of an investment or business venture. Each of these threats can be survived; the key is to look for the opportunity in the crisis when it happens. My father died at age sixty-four, and at the time, I took stock of the lessons of his life. The things I admired, I emulated; the things I didn't, I made sure not to repeat. I chose to take a significantly different path than he had.

Make a list of any family issues down the left-hand side of a page, and across the top write the words "Now," "Where," and "How." Take each of the issues, and write a few words about your "now" situation. Then write a brief description for each on "where" you want to be in, say, six months. The final step is to work out "how" you will bridge the gap between the "now" and the "where." This will become your family plan. Remember that family always comes first. If in doubt about what to do, just do what's best for the family, and manage the consequences of whatever that is.

What You Can Do Today—Family Must Come First

1. Make a list of your current family issues.
2. Describe where you are now, where you want to be, and how you will get there for each issue.

Chapter 49

● ● ●

Be the Head Coach, Not the Star Player

We start out in life with few competencies and many needs. We look up to and learn from those people in our lives who are more skilled and experienced than we are. Gradually, we become independent, with aspirations to become a golf pro, a policeman, or an astronaut. We want to be the star player. As we build our capabilities, the reality of just how difficult it is to be that star player kicks in. We compromise our ambitions, learning from our elders who have also compromised their ambitions. Nowhere in our aspirations is the head coach role.

As we build capability in walking and talking, feeding ourselves, and making friends, we have successes and failures along the way. We start our formal schooling, and we are forced to build capability in such areas as mathematics, language, writing, sports, and generally fitting into society. We find that mathematics is not easy, so we convince ourselves that our future is in the arts. Often school encourages participation, not winning or being the best. Even I got an award in my second year of high school for being the "Most Worthy." I still have that award.

We learn that participation means just turning up, being physically there if not mentally. The people who get all the rewards and recognition are the stars, the top of the class in mathematics, the fastest athlete, and the captain of the basketball team. There is little opportunity to be a coach, and no one teaches us how to be one. There is never any education in how to be a better leader; it is all about being a better follower.

We get our first jobs, and the process starts all over again; the rewards come for being a good follower. I think I was a good follower, but I wanted to be the best follower. The best boss in my life was a guy in South Australia who pulled me aside when I was twenty-five years old and told me that I was too conscientious and that I needed to wind back my dedication and enthusiasm. At age thirty-three, I had a different boss who told me I needed to switch off my A+—his version of telling me to wind back my dedication and enthusiasm.

Fighting against this pressure to be a good follower was a bit like fighting gravity. My response was to continue to be dedicated and enthusiastic but to hide it from my bosses. Instead of working late at the office, I worked at home. When I was thirty-four, I had a new job, and because my boss lived in a different state, I saw him only occasionally. I could be myself. It was around then that I started learning to be a head coach. I delegated whatever I could to my small team, and they were happy because that enriched their job roles and increased their job satisfaction.

My next job meant a move to Melbourne and a relatively large team of people spread over four countries. This role enabled me to be an even better head coach. I then discovered leverage. To get more leverage, you need to add technology or people, and preferably both. You need to transfer some of the things you are an expert in to others and take on leadership roles such as planning, directing, and coaching. Initially, your capability in these tasks will be low, and so it is tempting to revert back to your previous role where you got regular recognition and rewards. You need to recognize that your time as a star player is over; you need to become the head coach.

Remember how you became a star player in the first place, and apply the same process to becoming a head coach. It will require activities such as training, learning from better players, making mistakes, not giving up, and believing you will get better. Now apply the same steps to becoming a head coach. This is the end game, because regardless of how high you move up the leadership food chain, coaching will remain a key part of your job. I am currently coaching around 120 senior people, and I expect that number to grow. I am leveraged by my use of technology, most of which is provided by the Mindshop online platform that each of my 120 clients uses to communicate with me and to learn how to use the Mindshop tools.

To be good at anything involves activities such as education and training, learning from better operators than you, competing with people who are better than you, making mistakes and learning from them, not giving up, being prepared to pivot if need be, and having the self-belief that you can do it. Part of learning from better operators is being coached yourself. I receive my coaching from a team of people that includes some of my peers. I am part of a Mindshop leaders' group and receive continuous feedback and support from the other members of that group. I also get coached by some of my clients. They see me from a customer perspective, and that context is invaluable.

The key to becoming an effective head coach is to be a sponge—a sponge for learning, a sponge for feedback, and a sponge for change. If there is one other key, it would be adopting a "value to others" approach to everyone you meet. Just before Mindshop's Christmas party one year, I had another appointment beforehand, so I asked my wife, Julie, to pick me up on her way to the party. Traffic problems meant that was not going to work, so I booked an Uber car instead.

The Uber arrived within a few minutes. I got into the front seat next to the driver and said to him, "I figure we have about twenty-five minutes together, and I am a business coach. I don't meet anyone by accident. You must have a business—so how can I help you?"

His startled reply was, "I work in security, but I plan to set up a vending machine business to supplement my income. I have a lot of questions if you have the time." I was a captive audience for the next twenty-five minutes, and I coached him on whether to accept credit cards or cash only and on locations, risks, and what he needed to do about his own capability.

It was a win-win twenty-five minutes: I felt good about helping him, and he got free advice from an experienced business coach. The key point is that once you are a "head coach," you are always on duty. Keep your antennae up; everyone needs your help. Being paid is secondary.

What You Can Do Today—Be the Head Coach, Not the Star Player

1. Educate yourself about the tools and processes of coaching.
2. Learn by being coached by a head coach. Look for any opportunity to coach others (even in an Uber), and be proud of being a coach.

Chapter 50

● ● ●

Be Lean and Agile

The Japanese word for lean is *kaizen*. I became a devotee of kaizen around 1987; in fact, at that time, I purchased a vanity plate that said "KAIZEN" for one of my cars. To me, kaizen means "continuous improvement, all the time, using all the people." Kaizen has been a significant competitive advantage for Mindshop and all my clients. My first step when working with a business is to look at where we can remove waste.

The more waste you remove from an organization, the more efficient and profitable it is. The efficiency is good for your customers, and profit is good for shareholders. Waste or fat in the business is often intentionally built into an organization to compensate for its inefficient processes. If I am a manufacturer and I am not confident in the quality of my product or my ability to deliver the product on time, then I will build in excess stock of my products. It is not easy to change the organizational thinking around waste.

When I decided to adopt kaizen into Mindshop, I thought deeply about how to lock it in. I knew that if I publicly promised to do something for the important people in my life, I would not be able to fail. At the same time, I was using another Mindshop tool called Product Portfolio Analysis. Using this tool, it became clear that if I could significantly reduce the price point customers paid to join Mindshop, I would gain a strong and sustainable competitive advantage. It would only be sustainable if my competitors could not copy me.

What I decided to do was drop my price by 40 percent and never increase it again. Everyone thought I was mad. The advantage was that I had kaizen, which I could use to continuously pull cost from the business, a largely digital product, and my competitors would have difficulty emulating my processes, in part because I already had a critical mass of customers.

That is now more than twenty years ago, and we have maintained the promise ever since. The price has gone up in one country (due to exchange-rate movements) but only for new customers, and their price is also locked in for life. The philosophy of kaizen ensures that big results come from small changes over a long time, and I can proudly look back over the past twenty years and have confidence for the next twenty years.

Another essential trait is agility. In my mind, the key to agility is to have a crystal-clear vision for your business but with a willingness to keep changing how you will achieve that vision. Our vision is largely unchanged since we founded Mindshop. The consultants at McKinsey believe that agility requires a stable framework upon which dynamic capability is built. A cell-phone analogy helps explain the difference. The phone itself is the stable foundation (it doesn't change often), but it is the apps on that phone that provide the dynamic capability (they change regularly as needs arise). It is the integration of the two that enables you to be both lean and agile.

Agility often requires small numbers of people. Larger organizations are usually about as agile as a big ocean liner; they take a long time to change direction. Mindshop is more like my jet ski: fast, maneuverable, and precise. We use our most experienced customers to do most of our coaching, we contract out many of our core tasks to specialists, and our leaders focus on two things: strategy and customer service.

It is no accident that I don't work at the Mindshop office; I need to be out in the field dealing with customers, hearing and experiencing the problems and opportunities they have on a daily basis. Before the advent of e-mail, computers, and low-cost videoconferencing, I was literally in the field 90 percent of the time. Today it is more like a third of my time in the field, a third talking to clients using the emerging technology, and a third building solutions to what I learn while being in the field. This ensures that we are agile.

Another key ingredient is simplicity. Most, if not all, of our competitors seem to prefer a flashy front-of-house display, lots of salespeople, and mass marketing. As a result, they have massive churn of their customers. Mindshop is the opposite of all this in our desire to keep it very simple. We have a low-key office (still in a great location), regional managers who also do sales, sales built on referrals and repeat business, and very little customer churn.

Our stability is achieved by having a constant business model. Our competitors, in comparison, appear to be in constant change—changing their markets, their customers, their products, and their services. They appear and disappear; the people are the same, but they are slowly moving out of our market space each time they reincarnate their businesses. I shake my head at the waste, but we consider them to be helpful to us because they raise awareness yet lack capability. Their disenchanted customers, with their whetted appetites, ask around to find a replacement, and their peers recommend us. Our strong position in our market comes from being lean and agile, with the ability to pivot quickly but remain aligned to our long-term vision.

What You Can Do Today—Be Lean and Agile

1. The first step is to be lean; the Japanese call it kaizen. Research the words "lean" and "kaizen."

2. Continuously remove waste from your business.
3. The next step is to make sure you are agile. You, like a cell phone, need a stable foundation (the phone) and dynamic capability (the apps). Leanness and agility come from the apps. Develop plans for your dynamic capability.

Chapter 51

● ● ●

Learn What's Coming around the Bend

Until recently, one of my hobbies was racing road cars on a track. The competition was less about beating the other drivers and more about improving my personal time on the track. I retired having achieved good, if not great, personal best times for three of the iconic Australian racetracks: Phillip Island, Sandown, and Mount Panorama. One of the lessons you learn from your driving coaches is to keep your vision up. The natural tendency is to look at the entry to the next bend. You will not achieve your best time with that approach. You need to look around the bend and let your subconscious worry about the immediate concerns around speed, position on the track, braking, and acceleration. The good thing about racing on a track over, say, ten laps is that the track is generally the same for each of the laps. The only variations are limited to traffic and occasionally weather.

With life, particularly business life, there is little opportunity to keep going around the same circuit. Even if you could, the variations are significant: the economy, new competitors joining in, markets being redefined, and the like. In any case, you still need to keep your vision up and be less concerned about the next corner and more concerned about the strategy for the next three corners. Too often, leaders worry about the bends behind them, using the financial reports from the last month rather than looking forward. That is like me racing on a track but only looking at my rearview mirrors—or even worse, driving in the dark with no headlights switched on. The only certainty in either situation is that I will crash.

I was in a meeting with members of a client firm last year, and all the participants were senior experienced and clever people. I became frustrated that we were talking more about the past than the future, so I said, "Everyone is in this room because they are male, over fifty years of age, and used to be good at something. The problem with that is that what you used to be good at has nothing to do with the future. We need to be talking about things like artificial intelligence, virtual reality, augmented reality, and machine learning. What are you doing about learning these emerging technologies?"

My point was that we needed to be looking three corners ahead on our chosen track. We also needed to improve our capability in anticipating what the variables on our track were likely to be. In a business context, this can mean likely disruption from globalization and technology, loss of a key customer or employee, a new entrant to our market, or even the sale of the business to a competitor. So how do we get better at this?

In the case of the meeting just described, the composition of the team was a factor; we needed more diversity of views, knowledge, and experience. This firm was an active participant in its industry body. Its members were early adopters and leaders in their industry of technology. They did so well in so many areas, but they needed to improve their learning about what was coming around the corner. It is actually simpler than you think.

I am an avid user of Flipboard. Flipboard is primarily an online magazine aggregator with content that you can design by selecting components from a large menu of topics. I have currently selected components such as coaching and psychology, understanding psychology, home automation, *Tesla* magazine, accounting news and trends, and technology. People submit articles, Twitter links, and news items, and my magazine compiles articles from all my selected components. I access Flipboard several times a day because my magazine is continuously being updated as people submit material. I use Flipboard to assist me in looking around the corner in my areas of interest.

I am also an avid user of audiobooks that I purchase via the Amazon subsidiary Audible. I have a monthly subscription that gives me a free book of my choice each month. Each book is around eight hours of listening. I listen when exercising, when flying, and often when I am driving. I save each book to my Apple devices. To give you a feel for what I am listening to, some of my book titles and authors are as follows:

* *The Industries of the Future*—Alec Ross
* *Custom Design Your Own Destiny*—Bruce Goldberg
* *Ego Is the Enemy*—Ryan Holiday
* *The Third Wave*—Steve Case
* *Multipliers*—Liz Wiseman and Greg McKeown

These are just a few of the books I have listened to in the past year. If I like a particular book, I will buy the paperback version as well. I find the hard copy easier to flip through to find specific sections.

I also buy a lot of e-books via Amazon to read using a Kindle app on my Apple devices, even my smartphone. For me, e-books are an option halfway between audio and paperback books. These e-books tend to be books someone recommends to me or those I read or hear about, and I want them immediately. I can normally get an e-book in just a few minutes. Some of the books I have in this format, along with their authors, are the following:

* *Profit Is Not a Dirty Word*—Phillip Coombs
* *Mindset*—Carol Dweck
* *Rise of the Robots*—Martin Ford
* *The Challenger Customer*—Brent Adamson and Matthew Dixon
* *Constructing Grounded Theory*—Kathy Charmaz

The books and Flipboard are a key part of my keeping aware of what the future may bring. Everything is an opportunity, but you need to be ready to leverage these opportunities. I share my reading with others as they do with me. It takes time, but I choose to make this time. Although I am not a futurist, I do focus more on what is coming than I do on what has been.

What You Can Do Today—Learn What's Coming around the Bend

1. Load some books and magazines about the future onto your tablet or smartphone. Set a goal of consuming (on average) a book a month.
2. Keep a journal (I use my iPad) to record all the good ideas you will generate.

Chapter 52

● ● ●

Boost Your Probability of Success

Did you know that the probability of successfully implementing change is only 30 percent? This fact, and it is a fact,[1] means that to be successful, you need the tenacity to continue trying to make the change happen until you succeed. Most people can do that, but some give up after the first failure or two. Some of these people then refuse to try anything new because they are convinced they will fail.

No matter which of these groups you are in, the cost of only having a 30 percent probability of success is huge, both in financial and in nonfinancial terms. At the time when I was considering what problem I was going to research and develop a new theory on for my PhD, I observed how failure to change was having disastrous effects on some people I knew. My research goal was to develop a methodology that people could use to increase their probability of success to a much higher level. I figured that even if I only got it to 60 percent, that would be amazing.

I won't bore you with how I conducted the research, but the bottom line was to pick nine organizations, determine which were the best at implementing

---

1 A. A. Armenakis and S. G. Harris, "Reflections: Our Journey in Organizational Change Research and Practice," *Journal of Change Management* 9, no. 2 (2009): 127–42.

change, and then measure scientifically what the change success levels were. The second part of the research was to determine what they were specifically doing that resulted in that high level of success.

What came out of the research back in 2014 were three factors: the readiness for change, the capability of the people and the organization, and the beliefs of the people in that organization. The exciting finding was that the best organizations were achieving an 80 percent probability of success; the interesting point was that none of the leaders of these organizations knew how they were doing it.

The research findings, which drew on the work of other researchers in the areas of readiness and capability, listed five components of readiness, two of capability, and three of beliefs. In practical terms, what this meant for leaders was that if they could improve their performance in these ten components, they were likely to increase their probability of success in a change initiative from 30 percent to 80 percent. It seemed too good to be true, but with three years' experience in applying this new change-success theory at Mindshop, we are certain it works.

The change-readiness factors are often ignored in the haste of implementing the solution to the specific problem to be solved. The five factors are as follows:

1. Providing leadership support for the initiative.
2. Reaching agreement from the people that there is a need for the change.
3. Identifying a personal benefit for those implementing the change.
4. Establishing a belief that the actual change process being used is the most appropriate.
5. Developing confidence in the organization (both the self-confidence of each person and confidence in the organization to drive the change).

Don't expect to understand how to apply these factors; for now, it is enough just to know what they are.

The biggest of the three factors is capability. The capability factors are as follows:

1. Building capability in the people through training, coaching, and maybe even recruiting the required capabilities.
2. Building the dynamic capability of the organization in areas such as sales process, coaching, leadership, and profit improvement (this was the biggest need among the three change-success factors).

The third factor, beliefs, had three components, as follows:

1. People need to believe that the level of difficulty in implementing the change initiative is manageable.
2. Their attitude to the change initiative needs to be positive.
3. The significant people in each person's life need to agree that the change initiative is important.

When reading the list of ten factors, think about a change initiative you are currently working on. Rate your current performance on each of the ten. You need to have addressed all ten factors to achieve an 80 percent probability of a successful implementation. When we do this with organizations, we normally find they are doing a good job on a few of the components, an average job on about half the components, and a bad job on the rest. This helps explain why the normal probability of success is only 30 percent.

What You Can Do Today—Boost Your Probability of Success

1. Review your current performance on each of the ten change-success components (shown below). Then devise ways to improve the low-scoring components.

Mindshop Change-Success Model

1. leadership support for the initiative
2. perceived need for the change
3. personal benefit understood in participating in the change process
4. belief that you are using the most appropriate change process
5. confidence in both self and the organization that you can do this
6. capability of the people
7. capability of the organization
8. manageable perceived degree of difficulty in the change initiative
9. attitude of the people toward the change initiative
10. belief in the change held by the significant others of the people involved

Making It Happen

Whether you have read just one chapter or the whole book, your challenge now is to make it happen. The fifty-two insights in this book are designed for you to read at a rate of one chapter or insight per week. This does not preclude reading more than one chapter at a time, but then you have the issue of finding the time and energy to do something with your newfound knowledge.

I have assumed that you as the reader have reasonable business and life experience to draw on. If you do, then most of the insights will make sense, perhaps even resonating with your own experiences. I hope you have found the concepts practical and useful. They have been developed more from raw experience than academic learning.

But academic learning has influenced some of the insights. In my early days as a consultant, I was open to all new ideas, with little regard for where and how the concepts were developed. Today I am responsible for making sure that any conclusions or insights are evidence based. At worst, the evidence comes from my own senses, and at best, it comes from applied research—that is, use of the experiences of large numbers of leaders that has resulted in new concepts and models.

I caution you on being too enthusiastic in your application of the insights. If others have not read or don't understand them, you may find that your peers are reluctant to support you. This is less of a problem if you are the leader, but engagement of your people is still a necessity in any successful change implementation. Move forward cautiously, and be satisfied in even partial change if you cannot achieve a complete transformation. You will have less resistance if you apply the insights to your own life, so why not start there?

The key success factor in my and Mindshop's life is value to others. We apply it to every decision we make, including the decision to write this book. We hope you get value from each chapter, but we will be just as happy if just one of the insights provides you lots of value. All the Mindshop facilitators practice value to others in their lives as well. We currently support more than one thousand people at Mindshop; in fact, more than four thousand people have been part of us since we founded the company. I have had the privilege of coaching many of these people.

If we can be of any help or support to you going forward, you can contact us via e-mail at VTO@mindshop.com. As you now know, we carry any wounded, so we would be happy to help any people who are attempting to implement any of these insights. On behalf of the team at Mindshop, I wish you well and hope we will meet one day.

Dr. Chris Mason
Founder and Chairman
Mindshop
www.mindshop.com

Appendix 1–Suggested Reading List

stood in front of my bookcases and intuitively selected the resources I felt had an impact on who I am today. I list them in no particular order as follows:

* *Outliers*, Malcolm Gladwell
* *The Magic Power of Self-Image Psychology*, Maxwell Maltz
* *You'll See It When You Believe It*, Dr. Wayne Dyer
* *How to Live on 24 Hours a Day*, Arnold Bennett
* *As a Man Thinketh*, James Allen*
* *Atlas Shrugged*, Ayn Rand
* *Multipliers*, Liz Wiseman and Greg McKeown
* *Start with Why*, Simon Sinek*
* *Elon Musk*, Ashlee Vance
* *The Future of the Professions*, Richard and Daniel Susskind
* *The Challenger Sale*, Matthew Dixon, Brent Adamson, Pat Spenner, and Nick Toman*
* *The Challenger Customer*, Matthew Dixon, Brent Adamson, Pat Spenner, and Nick Toman
* *Great by Choice*, Jim Collins
* *Steve Jobs: The Exclusive Biography*, Walter Isaacson
* *Practicing Positive Psychology*, Robert Biswas-Diener

* *Think and Grow Rich*, Napoleon Hill*
* *The Lean Start-Up*, Eric Ries
* *Flow*, Mihaly Csikszentmihalyi
* *Spin Selling*, Neil Rackham*
* *Kaizen*, Masaaki Imai
* *Now Discover Your Strengths*, Marcus Buckingham and Donald O. Clifton
* *Theory of Constraints*, Eliyahu M. Goldratt
* *Sixth Sense*, Stuart Wilde

*My top five are marked.

Made in the USA
Lexington, KY
08 May 2017